Vignettes
from the Life of
'Abdu'l-Bahá

'Abdu'l-Bahá

Vignettes

from the Life of

'ABDU'L-BAHÁ

Collected and edited
by

Annamarie Honnold

GR

GEORGE RONALD
OXFORD

GEORGE RONALD, Publisher
46 High Street, Kidlington, Oxford, OX5 2DN

ISBN 0-85398-128-0 (cased)
ISBN 0-85398-129-9 (paper)

Printed in the United States of America

CONTENTS

Preface vii

Introduction I

I – His Pure Heart 9

II – His Kindly Heart 33

III – His Radiant Heart 109

Epilogue 158

Bibliography 175

References 180

Index to Anecdotes 191

Illustrations following pages 16, 48, 68, 104, 132 and 160

Dedicated
to
'Abdu'l-Bahá

PREFACE

Vignettes from the Life of 'Abdu'l-Bahá is not a biography, but a compilation of inspiring anecdotes pertaining to the Bahá'í way of life as demonstrated by 'Abdu'l-Bahá, the Son of the Founder of the Bahá'í Faith, Bahá'u'lláh, and the perfect Exemplar of His teachings. His words and deeds were in total harmony. His life – when known – serves to encourage and fortify His admirers, whether young or old, as they seek daily to follow the example He gave. And it was to this example that He called the Bahá'ís: '. . . guide ye the people and educate them in the ways of 'Abdu'l-Bahá. . . . Follow in the footsteps of 'Abdu'l-Bahá . . .'[1]

A number of reasons impelled me to write *Vignettes*. I had long felt a need for a concise book showing various aspects of 'Abdu'l-Bahá's character. This could, it seemed, best be done by recalling incidents in His life. To show how He was generous, for example, is more meaningful than simply to state that He was generous. To contemplate His happy, practical, yet divine way of living can guide us to greater satisfactions in our own lives, and fill today's spiritual void with meaning and certainty and joy. Indeed, the sooner we discover the truth of what life is all about, the sooner can we get on with the business of real living. All of us – children, youth and adults – need more than ever before a hero-figure, an Exemplar worth emulating. 'Abdu'l-Bahá best fills that need.

Stories about 'Abdu'l-Bahá are in great demand. Generally speaking, people enjoy anecdotes. But Bahá'í stories are found throughout a vast literature, going back for more than a century, and many of these publications are not readily available today. Having access to a number of the old books in English, I quite naturally felt impelled to bring together into one manuscript a selection of these inspiring incidents. They are presented simply, in no chronological order, and without the many delightful details which enhance biographical accounts.

Shoghi Effendi, Guardian of the Bahá'í Faith, counselled the American believers to remember the conduct of the Master: 'Let them call to mind, fearlessly and determinedly, the example and conduct of 'Abdu'l-Bahá while in their midst. Let them remember His courage, His genuine love, His informal and indiscriminating fellowship, His contempt for and impatience of criticism, tempered by His tact and wisdom. Let them revive and perpetuate the memory of those unforgettable and historic episodes and occasions on which He so strikingly demonstrated His keen sense of justice, His spontaneous sympathy for the down-trodden, His ever-abiding sense of the oneness of the human race, His overflowing love for its members, and His displeasure with those who dared to flout His wishes, to deride His methods, to challenge His principles, or to nullify His acts.'[2]

More recently, in 1966, the Universal House of Justice called particularly upon Bahá'í youth 'to develop their characters after the pattern of the Master . . .'[3] Some three years later this august body wrote, addressing the Bahá'ís of the world: 'In contemplating the Master's divine example we may well reflect that His life and deeds were not acted to a pattern of expediency, but were the inevitable and spontaneous expression of His inner self. We, likewise, shall act according to His example only as our inward spirits, growing and maturing through the disciplines of prayer and practice of the Teachings, become the wellsprings of all our attitudes and actions.'[4] And in 1974 the Universal House of Justice called for 'the development in the world-wide Bahá'í community of distinctive Bahá'í characteristics . . .'[5] These the Master demonstrated in abundance.

'Through an understanding of 'Abdu'l-Bahá as the Exemplar, or the "embodiment of every Bahá'í ideal", both adults and children can very quickly grasp the sense of Bahá'í law and develop the inner willingness to obey it. Of particular importance to children are the stories of 'Abdu'l-Bahá which show Him living the Bahá'í life and being obedient to the Covenant. If you are ever in doubt about how to behave in a given situation, meditate for a moment and then ask yourself, "What would the Master have done?"'[6] So wrote Dr Daniel Jordan.

Thus, the usefulness of stories is well recognized. Their spirit will hardly err. If there is error, it may rather lie in some small detail. Admittedly, the problem of authenticity is ever-present. The reference given will help the reader to determine if the story is authentic or in the class of pilgrims' notes – 'merely personal impressions of the sayings of their Master . . .'[7] It is well known that two people seeing the same event may give different versions of it. Then, too, details may be obscured by the passing of time. But because 'Abdu'l-Bahá is man's Exemplar for centuries to come, it is vital to know how He lived. A recorded story is more likely to retain its original form than one passed along by word of mouth for generations. If an anecdote quickens the reader's interest, or certain quotations seem to be out of context, the reference given may open the door to deeper understanding.

Other difficulties have been encountered. When does one stop the joyous process of research to begin the tedious labour of writing? The ocean is vast; the pearls are many. How does one choose the most beautiful? The most meaningful? But a start had to be made while there was yet time.

Some slight editing has been necessary, due in part to standardization in spelling and the transliteration of Persian names, since early Bahá'í publications. Also, capital letters have been added in old accounts, where necessary, for pronouns referring to Bahá'u'lláh and 'Abdu'l-Bahá. However, some inconsistencies do occur as I did not feel free to edit all quotations.

The book needed organization. The decision to portray 'Abdu'l-Bahá's character under three main headings – His Pure Heart, His Kindly Heart, and His Radiant Heart – was inspired by Bahá'u'lláh's first Arabic 'Hidden Word', which states: 'My first counsel is this: Possess a pure, kindly and radiant heart, that thine may be a sovereignty ancient, imperishable and everlasting.' It will be seen that one story might actually fit into different sections. For, in showing compassion, He could also portray generosity. The categories overlap – a story needed to be placed somewhere. The important thing is that He lived what He taught and in so doing showed us how to do the same.

The writer's own inadequacies might well have spelled total frustration and defeat. But has not 'Abdu'l-Bahá Himself told us we must not dwell on our own weakness? 'Do not look at thy weakness . . .'[8] He advised. It is actually presumptuous, indeed impossible, for any human being to attempt to do justice to a Spiritual Genius of the station of 'Abdu'l-Bahá.

Yet, may this little book diffuse divine fragrances. May it serve as an easily available collection of dearly-loved anecdotes about the Master, 'Abdu'l-Bahá. And may it sufficiently whet the spiritual appetite of the serious student to dig deeper into the many rich Bahá'í sources. May it also aid the earnest Bahá'í, whether young or old, when faced with a perplexing situation, to ask himself, 'What would 'Abdu'l-Bahá do?' and to find the answer. In so far as these hopes are realized *Vignettes* will have served its purpose – to bring the Master into our daily lives and to inspire us to emulate His 'divine art of living'.

My love for 'Abdu'l-Bahá runs deep. He blessed my sister, Margaret K. Ruhe, and me when He revealed a prayer for us while our parents, Dr and Mrs Jakob Kunz, were on pilgrimage in 1921. He desired us to grow 'in the mother-pearl of Bahá'í education'.[9] This education conferred both joy and meaning to our lives. With a sense of deep appreciation, I hope this modest contribution will help us all as we strive to foster Bahá'í ideals within ourselves and others.

I am deeply grateful to my mother, Anna Kunz, who led me to spiritual birth. And I greatly appreciate the part my husband, John, has played in encouraging me to get on with this book and in making it possible for me to do so. I should also like to thank Jeremy Fox and Marion Hofman for their expert editorial work.

Full details of the titles quoted, with their authors and publishers, are given in the References and Bibliography, with my grateful acknowledgement to all who have permitted their use. Without these many sources – publications and people – this book could never have been written. Profound is my gratitude to the many who took the time and gave the love to record for posterity their personal experiences.

ANNAMARIE K. HONNOLD

Swarthmore, Pennsylvania
1982

INTRODUCTION

The following is a brief outline of some of the main features of the life of 'Abdu'l-Bahá. It is intended primarily for those readers who are not already fairly well acquainted with His life-story and for whom some further background information may be helpful in appreciating how these various anecdotes fit in with the different stages of His life.

'Abdu'l-Bahá was born in Ṭihrán shortly before midnight on 22 May 1844 – the same night that the Báb,* in Shíráz, declared His Mission to Mullá Ḥusayn, the first to believe in Him. He was born into a wealthy Iranian family. His grandfather was a minister of state.

Soon after His birth, His Father, Bahá'u'lláh, received a scroll from the Báb whose God-given Mission He instantly acknowledged, becoming one of its most able promoters. This decision soon led to a dramatic change in circumstances for all the family.

Following the tragic martyrdom of the Báb in 1850 an attempt was made on the life of the Sháh by two Bábís, crazed with grief and holding him responsible for the Báb's death. This released an outbreak of extraordinary brutality and fanaticism throughout Írán directed against all suspected of being followers of the Báb. At this point, when 'Abdu'l-Bahá was but nine years old, Bahá'u'lláh was thrown into a dungeon in Ṭihrán, His home

---

* An independent Manifestation of God in His own right, the Báb was at the same time the 'Prophet-Herald' of Bahá'u'lláh's Revelation. The Báb's declaration of His mission marks the first year of the Bahá'í calendar.

plundered and His family forced to go into hiding in the capital city – their life never to be the same again.

During the time of this imprisonment 'Abdu'l-Bahá's Father had an experience which made Him aware that He was the One promised by the Báb, destined to become the World Redeemer. Taken one day to visit Bahá'u'lláh, 'Abdu'l-Bahá recalled how '. . . one day He was allowed to enter the prison yard to see His beloved father when He came out for His daily exercise. Bahá'u'lláh was terribly altered, so ill He could hardly walk, His hair and beard unkempt, His neck galled and swollen from the pressure of a heavy steel collar, His body bent by the weight of His chains, and the sight made a never-to-be-forgotten impression on the mind of the sensitive boy.'[1] It was during this time that 'Abdu'l-Bahá had His first direct experience of persecution, when He was pursued and stoned by youths because He was a 'Bábí'.

His innocence recognized, Bahá'u'lláh was nevertheless exiled from His native land, and went with His family to Baghdád in 1853 where they remained for the next ten years. The journey was hard, being made in winter with inadequate provisions – 'Abdu'l–Bahá's Father ill from His imprisonment and His mother pregnant. Twice 'Abdu'l-Bahá's toes froze, the effect of which He felt for the remainder of His life.

During the time in Baghdád, where grew a sizeable community of Bábís, mostly refugees from the persecutions in Persia, Bahá'u'lláh, like so many previous Founders of the world's religions, retired to the wilderness – in this case for two years to the mountains of Kurdistán – and no one knew where He was. At this time 'Abdu'l-Bahá, Bahá'u'lláh's eldest son and little more than a child, did much to support and give courage and hope to His mother and family.

By the time He returned home Bahá'u'lláh was already

becoming well-known for His holiness and wisdom. Growing numbers of people, quite apart from Bábís, began to flock to see Him, some in earnest and some out of curiosity. Increasingly 'Abdu'l-Bahá undertook to meet such people and only the truly sincere would He admit to His Father's presence. He associated with men of learning who marvelled at His knowledge and when they asked Him where He had acquired it, 'Abdu'l-Bahá would simply reply '. . . from my Father'.

Already, soon after their arrival in Baghdád, Bahá'u'lláh had privately told 'Abdu'l-Bahá of God's Revelation to Him and 'Abdu'l-Bahá had immediately believed in Him. In 1863, just prior to their banishment to Constantinople (now Istanbul), Bahá'u'lláh declared His Mission to those followers of the Báb gathered in the Garden of Riḍván either to bid Him farewell or to share His further exile. He was the World Redeemer promised by all the world's religions and announced by the Báb.

After only four months in Constantinople they were exiled for a further five years to Adrianople (now Edirne) where Bahá'u'lláh publicly proclaimed His Mission to the world's leaders, both ecclesiastical and secular, in a series of now famous letters.

Finally, in 1868, they were exiled a fourth time, on this occasion to 'Akká, then a foul and fever-ridden city in Palestine (now Israel). There they spent the first two years in the 'Most Great Prison', followed by a further seven years within the city walls in a state of virtual house-arrest, still prisoners within the prison-city. It was during this time that 'Abdu'l-Bahá was married.

From the time of their arrival in 'Akká, Bahá'u'lláh increasingly relied on 'Abdu'l-Bahá, to whom He always referred as the 'Master', for all dealings with officials and the public. By 1877 such was the respect and admiration for both Bahá'u'lláh and the Master that, despite the fact

3

that they were officially supposed to be kept in the strictest confinement, the Governor permitted Bahá'u'-lláh and His family to move out to live in the countryside, ✓ where Bahá'u'lláh eventually passed away in 1892 in the Mansion of Bahjí.

In His Will Bahá'u'lláh had made 'Abdu'l-Bahá the Centre of His Covenant – to Him all the Bahá'ís should turn for guidance. He was to be the sole Interpreter of His Father's teachings, the perfect 'Exemplar of His faith' and the 'Shepherd of His flock'. To Him the orphaned Bahá'í community turned, recognizing in Him '. . . its Solace, its Guide, its Mainstay and Champion'.[2]

✓ Sadly, the half-brother of 'Abdu'l-Bahá, along with a number of other close relatives, was so overcome by jealousy of the exalted position given 'Abdu'l-Bahá in His Father's Will that it aroused in him an envy '. . . as deadly as that which the superior excellence of Joseph had kindled in the hearts of his brothers, as deep-seated as that which had blazed in the bosom of Cain and prompted him to slay his brother Abel . . .'[3] While this failed to create any permanent breach in the unity of the Bahá'í community it caused 'Abdu'l-Bahá much personal anguish and suffering, as is indicated in some of the following anecdotes.

During those last few remaining years of the nineteenth century 'Abdu'l-Bahá began to dispatch teachers to America, as well as to the East, and by the turn of the century a growing stream of pilgrims from the West began to arrive to see 'Abdu'l-Bahá. This continued almost until the outbreak of World War I.

✓ The Young Turk Revolution in 1908, which led to the freeing of all political and religious prisoners in the Ottoman Empire, marked another turning point in 'Abdu'l-Bahá's life. Thus, after forty years' confinement in Palestine, 'Abdu'l-Bahá was to enjoy freedom of movement and was able to plan His momentous pre-war

journeys of 1911 and 1912–13 through Europe and
America, proclaiming and explaining His Father's
Message.

An indication of the interest His visit to the West
aroused can be gauged from these words of Lady
Blomfield, in whose house 'Abdu'l-Bahá stayed, in
London. 'O, these pilgrims, these guests, these visitors!
Remembering those days, our ears are filled with the
sound of their footsteps – as they came from every
country in the world. Every day, all day long, a constant
stream, an interminable procession!

'Ministers and missionaries, oriental scholars and
occult students, practical men of affairs and mystics,
Anglicans, Catholics, and Non-conformists, Theosophists and Hindus, Christian Scientists and doctors of
medicine, Muslims, Buddhists and Zoroastrians. There
also called: politicians, Salvation Army soldiers, and
other workers for human good, women suffragists,
journalists, writers, poets and healers, dressmakers and
great ladies, artists and artisans, poor workless people
and prosperous merchants, members of the dramatic and
musical world, these all came; and none were too lowly,
nor too great, to receive the sympathetic consideration of
this holy Messenger, Who was ever giving His life for
others' good.'[4]

Thus, in 1912, having previously visited London and
Paris, after a winter in Egypt, 'Abdu'l-Bahá, despite
ill-health and His age (now 68 years old), carried out an
exacting programme of proclamation of the Message of
Bahá'u'lláh, travelling from one coast of the United
States to the other as well as north into Canada. '. . . in
the city of New York alone He delivered public addresses
in, and made formal visits to, no less than fifty-five
different places. Peace societies, Christian and Jewish
congregations, colleges and universities, welfare and
charitable organizations, members of ethical cults, New

Thought centers, metaphysical groups, Women's clubs, scientific associations, gatherings of Esperantists, Theosophists, Mormons, and agnostics, institutions for the advancement of the colored people, representatives of the Syrian, the Armenian, the Greek, the Chinese, and Japanese communities – all were brought into contact with His dynamic presence, and were privileged to hear from His lips His Father's Message. Nor was the press either in its editorial comment or in the publication of reports of His lectures, slow to appreciate the breadth of His vision or the character of His summons.'[5] This was all the more remarkable when we realize that His first-ever public speech had been given from the pulpit of the City Temple in London the year before. He was to complete a further and more extensive tour of Europe on His way back to the Holy Land. Many of the anecdotes contained in this volume have their origin in these historic western journeys and a considerable number of the talks He gave during this trip are recorded in such books as *Paris Talks*, *Abdu'l-Baha in London*, *'Abdu'l-Bahá in Canada*, and the two-volume *Promulgation of Universal Peace* containing one hundred and thirty-nine talks given in the United States and Canada.

After the War, pilgrims again found their way to Palestine to visit the Master in Haifa where He had His home at the foot of Mount Carmel, not far from the Shrine of the Báb.

In 1920 a Knighthood of the British Empire was conferred on Him for His efforts to relieve the suffering of the inhabitants of Palestine during the arduous days of World War I.

'Abdu'l-Bahá maintained a staggering world-wide correspondence, being known to write as many as ninety letters in a day and '. . . to pass many a night, from dusk to dawn, alone in His bed-chamber engaged in a correspondence which the pressure of His manifold responsibilities had prevented Him from attending to in the day-time.'[6] The World Centre has over 19,000 original and authenticated copies of His letters.

One of the outstanding fruits resulting from these western journeys was His series of letters to the American believers, known as the *Tablets of the Divine Plan*, His charter for all future teaching plans destined to establish the Bahá'í Faith throughout the world.

Within the context of such a momentous life, what, in addition to those already mentioned, were 'Abdu'l-Bahá's main achievements? Firstly, the preservation of the unity of the world-wide Bahá'í community, not only in His own lifetime, but into the future, through the clarity of His instructions contained in His Will and Testament, a momentous document 'which called into being, outlined the features and set in motion the processes'[7] of the administrative structure of the Faith to be developed after His passing. He managed, against all odds, to carry out Bahá'u'lláh's instructions to transfer the remains of the Báb from Írán to the Holy Land and bury them in a Shrine on Mount Carmel on the very spot Bahá'u'lláh had indicated. He initiated the building of the first two Bahá'í Houses of Worship – the first in Russian Turkistán, the second in the United States. He fully warned the world's leaders and thinkers of the dangers and obstacles to world peace and laid out the measures prescribed by Bahá'u'lláh in order to render peace possible, through the establishment of a New World Order.

When He passed away in 1921, ten thousand people, representing a wide variety of different races, classes and religions, came out to pay their final tributes. His was '. . . a funeral the like of which Haifa, nay Palestine itself, had surely never seen; so deep was the feeling that brought so many thousands of mourners together . . .

'The High Commissioner of Palestine, Sir Herbert

Samuel, the Governor of Jerusalem, the Governor of Phoenicia, the Chief Officials of the Government, the Consuls of the various countries, resident in Haifa, the heads of the various religious communities, the notables of Palestine, Jews, Christians, Moslems, Druses, Egyptians, Greeks, Turks, Kurds, and a host of His American, European and native friends, men, women and children, both of high and low degree, all, about ten thousand in number, mourning the loss of their Beloved One.'[8]

His was a lifetime of unstinting service to God, to God's latest Manifestation to mankind – Bahá'u'lláh – and to humanity, whose ultimate high destiny He never ceased to affirm. His life is remarkable for the harmony between His words and His deeds. It is of historical importance to the world not only because of the vital role He played in the effective establishment of God's latest Revelation on earth, but also because His example and teachings continue to live and exercise their influence in the daily lives of those growing millions of Bahá'ís throughout the world for whom He is both the perfect example of the 'divine art of living' and a 'shelter for all mankind'.[9]

For a more comprehensive account of the life of 'Abdu'l-Bahá the reader is particularly referred to the biography *'Abdu'l-Bahá* by H. M. Balyuzi and appropriate sections of *God Passes By* by Shoghi Effendi, Guardian of the Bahá'í Faith and grandson of 'Abdu'l-Bahá. Details of these and other books will be found in the bibliography at the back of this volume.

Chapter I

HIS PURE HEART

Today the most pressing of all tasks is the purification of character, the reforming of morals, the rectification of conduct.[1]

The pure heart is one that is entirely cut away from self. To be selfless is to be pure.[2]

'Abdu'l-Bahá

Selflessness

I

At Wandsworth Prison the Master, 'Abdu'l-Bahá, wrote in the visitors' book: 'The greatest prison is the prison of self.'[3]

2

When people said to 'Abdu'l-Bahá how happy they were that He was now free, He replied:

'Freedom is not a matter of place, but of condition. I was happy in that prison, for those days were passed in the path of service.

'To me prison was freedom.

'Troubles are a rest to me.

'Death is life.

'To be despised is honour.

9

'Therefore was I full of happiness all through that prison time.

'When one is released from the prison of self, that is indeed freedom! For self is the greatest prison.

'When this release takes place one can never be imprisoned.

'Unless one accepts dire vicissitudes, not with dull resignation, but with radiant acquiescence, one cannot attain this freedom.'[4]

3

'Abdu'l-Bahá was once asked, 'What is Satan?' He replied in three words: 'The insistent self'. [5]

4

When a reporter of the New York *Globe* visited 'Abdu'l-Bahá in Haifa, He gave her this message: 'Tell my followers that they have no enemies to fear, no foes to hate. Man's only enemy is himself.'[6]

5

'Abdu'l-Bahá had this to say of selfishness: 'Self-love is a strange trait and the means of the destruction of many important souls in the world. If man be imbued with all good qualities but be selfish, all the other virtues will fade or pass away and eventually he will grow worse.'[7]

6

The first person singular seldom crept into the Master's speech. He once told a group of New York friends that in the future the words 'I' and 'Me' and 'Mine' would be regarded as profane.[8]

7

In 1914 *The Christian Commonwealth* carried words of praise for 'Abdu'l-Bahá: 'It is wonderful to see the venerable figure of the revered Bahá'í leader passing through the narrow streets of this ancient town ['Akká], where he lived for forty years as a political prisoner, and to note the deep respect with which he is saluted by the Turkish officials and the officers of the garrison from the Governor downward, who visit him constantly and listen with the deepest attention to his words. "The Master" does not teach in Syria as he did in the West,* but he goes about doing good, and Mohammedans and Christians alike share his benefactions. From sunrise often till midnight he works, in spite of broken health, never sparing himself if there is a wrong to be righted or a suffering to be relieved. To Christians who regard 'Abdu'l-Bahá with impartial and sympathetic eyes, this wonderful selfless life cannot fail to recall that life whose tragic termination on Calvary the whole Christian world recalls . . .'[9]

---

* Bahá'u'lláh had promised the Turkish Government that the Bahá'ís would not teach the people of Palestine. The Master respected that promise. They taught only by example.[10]

8

Two pilgrims were at the Master's luncheon table one day in 1908. He asked them if they were glad to be in 'Akká and if they were happy. They replied that they were very happy to be there with Him, but unhappy when they thought of their own faults. 'Think not of yourselves,' He said, 'but think of the Bounty of God. This will always make you happy.' Then with a smile He referred to an Arabic saying about the peacock, who 'is contented because he never looks at his feet – which are very ugly – but always at his plumage which is very beautiful.'[11]

9

Only the Master, knowing the station bestowed upon Him by Bahá'u'lláh, could say, as He did: '. . . look at Me, follow Me, be as I am; take no thought for yourselves or your lives, whether ye eat or whether ye sleep, whether ye are comfortable, whether ye are well or ill, whether ye are with friends or foes, whether ye receive praise or blame; for all of these things ye must care not at all. Look at Me and be as I am; ye must die to yourselves and to the world, so shall ye be born again and enter the Kingdom of Heaven. Behold a candle how it gives its light. It weeps its life away drop by drop in order to give forth its flame of light.'[12]

10

The Master's life was centered on God, not on Himself. To do God's will, to be His servant, were His concerns.

He disliked photographs of Himself, permitting them only to satisfy His friends. 'But to have a picture of oneself,' He said, 'is to emphasise the personality, which is merely the lamp, and is quite unimportant. The light burning within the lamp has the only real significance.'[13]

II

'Abdu'l-Bahá was not afraid of silence; indeed, He knew its virtue. Howard Colby Ives has recalled: 'To the questioner He responded first with silence – an outward silence. His encouragement always was that the other should speak and He listen. There was never that eager tenseness, that restlessness so often met showing most plainly that the listener has the pat answer ready the moment he should have a chance to utter it.'[14] And Ives recounts a charming story about another Unitarian minister* who was interviewing 'Abdu'l-Bahá for an article on the Bahá'í Faith. His questions were long. The Master listened 'with unwearied attention', replying mostly in monosyllables, but relaxed and interested. A great 'understanding love' flowed from Him to the minister. Ives grew impatient, but not the Master; His guest must be heard fully. When at last His questioner paused, after a brief silence 'Abdu'l-Bahá spoke to him with wisdom and love, calling him 'my dear son'. Within five minutes the minister 'had become humble, for the moment, at least, a disciple at His feet. . . . Then 'Abdu'l-Bahá rose . . . lovingly embraced the doctor and led him towards the door. At the threshold He paused. His eyes had lighted upon a large bunch of American Beauty roses . . . He laughed aloud . . . stooped, gathered the whole bunch in His arms . . . and

* Mr Ives himself was at that time a Unitarian minister.

placed them all in the arms of His visitor. Never shall I forget that round, bespectacled, grey head above that immense bunch of lovely flowers. So surprised, so radiant, so humble, so transformed.'[15]

12

One day 'Abdu'l-Bahá was going from 'Akká to Haifa and asked for a seat in the stage coach. The driver, surprised, said 'Your Excellency surely wishes a private carriage.' 'No,' replied the Master. While He was still in the coach in Haifa, a distressed fisherwoman came to Him; all day she had caught nothing and now must return to her hungry family. The Master gave her five francs, then turned to the driver and said: 'You now see the reason why I would not take a private carriage. Why should I ride in luxury when so many are starving?'[16]

13

During 'Abdu'l-Bahá's last days in America, the Bahá'ís were eager to show their love and gratitude by contributions of money, but these He refused. 'I am pleased with your services,' He told them, 'and I am grateful for all you have done for Me. . . . Now you have brought presents for the members of My family. They are acceptable, but the best of all presents is the love of God which remains preserved in the treasuries of hearts. Material presents remain for a time but this lasts forever. These presents require chests and shelves for safe keeping while this is preserved in the repositories of the minds and hearts and remains eternal and immortal forever in the divine worlds. I shall, therefore, convey to them your love which is the most precious of all gifts. No one uses diamond rings in our home and no one wants rubies. That house is free from all these things.

'I, however, accept your presents but I leave them in your safe keeping with the request that you will kindly sell them and send the proceeds to the funds for the Ma_sh_riqu'l-A_dh_kár.'[17]

14

Whenever 'Abdu'l-Bahá discussed the importance of teaching the Bahá'í Faith He spoke with emphasis, and in His Will and Testament He wrote: 'Of all the gifts of God the greatest is the gift of Teaching.'[18]

'The disciples of Christ forgot themselves and all earthly things, forsook all their cares and belongings, purged themselves of self and passion and with absolute detachment scattered far and wide and engaged in calling the peoples of the world to the Divine Guidance, till at last they made the world another world . . . Let them that are men of action follow in their footsteps!'[19]

Humility

15

The Master's humility was shown in many ways. He desired no name or title except that of 'Abdu'l-Bahá – the Servant of God. He forbade pilgrims to fall at His feet. In the early days in 'Akká, He cooked for His fellow prisoners, and later, when entertaining visitors at His table, He sometimes served His guests Himself, 'a practice he recommended to other hosts'.[20]

16

When Bahá'u'lláh lived at Bahjí – and 'Abdu'l-Bahá at 'Akká – the Master would visit His Father once a week. He liked to do this on foot and when asked why He did not ride to Bahjí He responded by asking, '. . . who am I that I should ride where the Lord Christ walked?'[21]

However, His Father requested Him to ride, so in order to comply the Master rode out of 'Akká, but when He sighted Bahá'u'lláh's Mansion, He dismounted.

Bahá'u'lláh used to watch out for His approach from His second-floor window and as soon as He saw Him coming, He would joyously tell His family to go out to meet Him.

17

During World War I when a blockade threatened the lives of many civilians in Haifa, 'Abdu'l-Bahá saved them from starvation. 'He personally organized extensive agricultural operations near Tiberias, thus securing a great supply of wheat . . .'[22] Food was stored in underground pits and elsewhere. This He distributed to the inhabitants, regardless of religion or nationality. The food was systematically rationed. Having started His preparations as early as 1912, He averted tragedy in the dark days of 1917 and 1918.

At war's end the British were quick to recognize His painstaking accomplishments. He was to be knighted on 27 April 1920, at the residence of the British Governor in Haifa at a ceremony held especially for Him. British and religious dignitaries came to honour Him on this auspicious occasion. His unselfish acts had won Him the love and respect of high and low alike. 'Abdu'l-Bahá

'Abdu'l-Bahá addressing the friends on the occasion of His laying
the cornerstone of the Bahá'í House of Worship, Wilmette, Illinois,
1 May 1912

'Abdu'l-Bahá on the way to the ceremony of investiture as a Knight of the British Empire, 27 April 1920

consented to accept the knighthood – but He was not impressed with worldly honour or ceremony. Even a formality must be simplified. An elegant car was sent to bring Him to the Governor's residence, but the chauffeur did not find the Master at His home. People scurried in every direction to find Him. Suddenly, He appeared '. . . alone, walking His kingly walk, with that simplicity of greatness which always enfolded Him.'[23]

Isfandíyár, His long-time faithful servant, stood near at hand. Many were the times when he had accompanied the Master on His labours of love. Now, suddenly, with this elegant car ready to convey his Master to the Governor, he felt sad and unneeded. Intuitively, 'Abdu'l-Bahá must have sensed this – He gave him a sign. Isfandíyár dashed off – the horse was harnessed, the carriage brought to the lower gate and the Master was driven to a side entrance of the garden of the Governor. Isfandíyár was joyous – he was needed even yet. Quietly, without pomp, 'Abbás Effendi arrived at the right time at the right place and did honour to those who would honour Him when He was made Sir 'Abdu'l-Bahá 'Abbás, K.B.E. – a title which He almost never used.[24]

18

Whenever possible 'Abdu'l-Bahá attempted to avoid unnecessary fanfare. Once, wealthy visitors from the West planned an elaborate pre-meal, hand-washing scene for Him – it included a page boy, a clean bowl with 'crystal water' and even a scented towel! When the Master saw the group walking across the lawn, He knew their purpose. He hurried to a small water-trough, washed as usual and then wiped His hands on the cloth of the gardener. Radiantly, He then turned to meet His guests. The preparations meant for Him He used for them.[25]

19

'Abdu'l-Bahá laid the cornerstone of the House of Worship in Wilmette, Illinois, on 1 May 1912. A temporary tent covered a spot of prairie overlooking Lake Michigan. People from different nationalities were on hand to ceremoniously turn over a bit of soil. An ordinary spade was used, but when the Master's turn came He was handed a golden trowel. He handed it back and used instead the same spade as the others. He then laid the cornerstone.[26]

20

'Abdu'l-Bahá inspired the creation of a Local Spiritual Assembly in New York City. Loulie Mathews, one of those present when the friends met to form their first local institution, recalled that they had very little idea of how to proceed. Anxious to impress each other they first sat stiffly along the wall. No, a circle would be better – so they moved. Suddenly the doorbell rang. Grace Krug returned with a cablegram – from 'Abdu'l-Bahá! It stated simply: 'Read Matthew, Chapter 19, Verse 30.' They needed a Bible. Finally both Bible and page were found. The message read, 'But many that are first shall be last; and the last shall be first.' 'Presto, we became as humble as mice – afraid lest that last place should be ours! 'Abdu'l-Bahá gave us a wonderful lesson that evening! If we went away without too much knowledge of how to form an Assembly, we learned a lesson in how to become

Bahá'ís. Bathed in the aura of humility the Assembly came into being.'[27]

21

'Abdu'l-Bahá's humility did not stem from any weakness. Once when a child asked Him why all the rivers of the earth flow into the ocean, He said, 'because it sets itself lower than them all and so draws them to itself.'[28]

22

In Philadelphia, 'Abdu'l-Bahá spoke to the friends about the Nineteen-Day Feast, which lies at the foundation of Bahá'í spiritual and community life and which is held at the start of each Bahá'í month. He stressed the importance of this occasion: 'Each one of you must think how to make happy and pleased the other members of your Assembly, and each one must consider all those who are present as better and greater than himself, and each one must consider himself less than the rest. Know their station as high, and think of your own station as low. Should you act and live according to these behests, know verily, of a certainty, that that Feast is the Heavenly Food. That Supper is the "Lord's Supper"! I am the Servant of that gathering.'[29]

23

Howard Ives wrote, 'In all of my many opportunities of meeting, of listening to and talking with 'Abdu'l-Bahá I was impressed, and constantly more deeply impressed, with His method of teaching souls. . . . He never argued, of course. Nor did He press a point. He left one free. There was never an assumption of authority, rather He was ever the personification of humility. He taught "as if offering a gift to a king." He never told me what I should do, beyond suggesting that what I was doing was right. Nor did He ever tell me what I should believe. He made Truth and Love so beautiful and royal that the heart perforce did reverence. He showed me by His voice, manner, bearing, smile, how I should *be*, knowing that out of the pure soil of being the good fruit of deeds and words would surely spring.'[30]

24

Mírzá Abu'l-Faḍl was an outstanding Bahá'í scholar. Early in this century the Master sent him to the United States of America both to teach and to help the believers to deepen. 'After his return, he and a number of American pilgrims were seated in the presence of 'Abdu'l-Bahá in 'Akká. The pilgrims began to praise Mírzá Abu'l-Faḍl for the help he had given them, saying that he had taught many souls, defended the Cause most ably against its adversaries, and had helped to build a strong and dedicated Bahá'í community in America. As they continued to pour lavish praise upon him, Mírzá Abu'l-Faḍl became increasingly depressed and dejected, until he burst into tears and wept loudly. The believers were surprised and could not understand this, even thinking that they had not praised him enough!

'Then 'Abdu'l-Bahá explained that by praising him they had bitterly hurt him, for he considered himself as utter nothingness in the Cause and believed with absolute sincerity that he was not worthy of any mention or praise.'[31]

Simplicity

25

One of the last pilgrims to visit 'Abdu'l-Bahá in the Holy Land in 1921 was Anna Kunz, the daughter of a Swiss theologian who lived in Zürich in Switzerland. She later recalled, 'As I think of him now, I always love to think, first, of his great simplicity, his marvelous humility which knows of no self-existence, and last, or better, first, of his boundless love.'[32]

26

The Master kept little clothing – one coat at a time was ample. He ate little food. He was known to begin His day with tea, goat's milk cheese and wheat bread. And at the evening meal a cup of milk and a piece of bread might suffice. He considered the latter a healthy meal. Had not Bahá'u'lláh, while at Sulaymáníyyih, subsisted mostly on milk? (Sometimes Bahá'u'lláh ate rice and milk cooked together.) 'Abdu'l-Bahá's sparse diet also included herbs and olives – it rarely included meat.

27

Mary Lucas, a pilgrim to 'Akká in 1905, found that the Master usually ate but one simple meal a day. In eight days He was present at most meals, often coming just to add joy to the occasion, though He was not hungry. If He knew of someone who had had no meal during a day, the family supper was gladly packed up and sent to the needy.[33]

28

On the occasion of 'Abdu'l-Bahá's first dinner in the home of Lady Blomfield in London His hostess had prepared course after course in her eagerness to please Him. Afterwards He gently commented: 'The food was delicious and the fruit and flowers were lovely, but would that we could share some of the courses with those poor and hungry people who have not even one.'[34] Thereafter, the dinners were greatly simplified. Flowers and fruit remained in abundance, for these were often brought to the Master as small love tokens.

29

Julia Grundy, an early pilgrim, described a beautiful supper at which many friends were welcomed by the Master Himself in 'Akká. He passed out napkins, embraced and found places for each. All were individually anointed with attar of rose. He served pilau,* a Persian rice dish, to each guest. There were also oranges and rice pudding. 'Throughout the supper, which was very simple in its character and appointment, 'Abdu'l-Bahá was the Servant of the believers. This was indeed a spiritual feast where Love reigned. The whole atmosphere was Love, Joy, and Peace.'[35]

* See ref. 35 for recipe.

30

May Bolles (Maxwell) took an early pilgrimage to the prison-city. She heard that the food man eats is of no importance, as its effect endures but a short time. But the food of the spirit is life to the soul and its effects endure eternally. She heard 'Abdu'l-Bahá tell the touching 'story of the hermit'. Bahá'u'lláh 'was travelling from one place to another with His followers' and 'He passed through a lonely country where, at some little distance from the highway, a hermit lived alone in a cave. He was a holy man, and having heard that Our Lord, Bahá'u'lláh, would pass that way, he watched eagerly for His approach. When the Manifestation arrived at that spot the hermit knelt down and kissed the dust before His feet, and said to Him: "Oh, my Lord, I am a poor man living alone in a cave nearby; but henceforth I shall account myself the happiest of mortals if Thou wilt but come for a moment to my cave and bless it by Thy Presence." Then Bahá'u'lláh told the man that He would come, not for a moment but for three days, and He bade His followers cast their tents, and await His return. The poor man was so overcome with joy and gratitude that he was speechless, and led the way in humble silence to his lowly dwelling in a rock. There the Glorious One sat with him, talking to him and teaching him, and toward evening the man bethought himself that he had nothing to offer his great Guest but some dry meat and some dark bread, and water from a spring nearby. Not knowing what to do he threw himself at the feet of his Lord and confessed his dilemma. Bahá'u'lláh comforted him and by a word bade him fetch the meat and bread and water; then the Lord of the universe partook of this frugal repast with joy and fragrance as though it had been a banquet, and during the three days of His visit they ate only of this food which seemed to the poor hermit the most delicious he had ever eaten. Bahá'u'lláh declared that He had never been more nobly entertained nor received greater hospitality and love. "This," exclaimed the Master, when He had finished the story, "shows us how little man requires when he is nourished by the sweetest of all foods – the love of God." '[36]

31

'Abdu'l-Bahá's family was taught to dress in such a way that they would be 'an example to the rich and an encouragement to the poor'.[37] Available money was stretched to cover far more than the Master's family needs. One of His daughters wore no bridal gown when she married – a clean dress sufficed. The Master was queried why He had not provided bridal clothes. With candour He replied simply, 'My daughter is warmly clad and has all that she needs for her comfort. The poor have not. What my daughter does not need I will give to the poor rather than to her.'[38]

32

The husband of Amelia Collins, a devoted American Bahá'í, was a very sociable man. He could take part in any discussion with perfect freedom and ease. But once, before entering the Master's home, he was so excited that he arranged his tie just right, smoothed his clothes and repeatedly asked his wife what he should do when they arrived there. She told him, 'Nothing! In the family of 'Abdu'l-Bahá simplicity reigns, and nothing but love is ever accepted.'[39]

33

'Abdu'l-Bahá had such an easy way of leading into a meaningful conversation. He would begin 'with some simple reference to a natural thing, the weather, food, a stone, tree, water, the prison, a garden or a bird, our coming, or some little act of service, and this base would be woven into a parable and teaching of wisdom and simplicity, showing the oneness of all Spiritual Truth, and adapting it always to the life, both of the individual and of mankind. All of His words are directed toward helping men to live. Unless questions of metaphysics, dogmas and doctrines be introduced, He seldom mentions them. He speaks easily, clearly, in brief phrases, each of which is a gem.'[40]

Cleanliness

34

The Master considered cleanliness of vital importance. He was indeed 'the essence of cleanliness' even as Bahá'u'lláh had taught His followers. Florence Khánum bore witness to this, for she found Him 'dazzlingly, spotlessly . . . shining, from snowy turban-cloth, to white, snowy hair falling upon His shoulders, to white snowy beard and long snowy garment . . . Although it was high noon, in summer . . . His attire was crisp and fresh-looking, as though He had not been visiting the sick, and in prison, and toiling for mankind since early morning. Often a deliciously fresh rose was tucked in His belt.'[41]

35

Not only His person but also His immediate surroundings needed to be spotless. Once when He had guests – whom He would always honour – He asked that the chimney of a lamp be replaced as it was not sufficiently polished.[42]

Patience

36

'There was a Christian merchant in 'Akká who, like many of his fellow-citizens, held the Bahá'ís in scant respect. It happened that he came upon a load of charcoal which some of the Bahá'ís had been permitted to buy outside 'Akká. (Inside the town they were denied such purchases.) The merchant, noticing that the fuel was of a fine grade, took it for his own use. For him Bahá'ís were beyond the pale, and so their goods could be impounded. When 'Abdu'l-Bahá heard of the incident, He went to the place where the merchant transacted his business to ask for the return of the charcoal. There were many people about in that office, bent on their trade, and they took no notice of 'Abdu'l-Bahá. He sat and waited. Three hours passed before the merchant turned to Him and said: "Are you one of the prisoners in this town?" 'Abdu'l-Bahá said that He was, and the merchant then enquired: "What was the crime for which you were imprisoned?" 'Abdu'l-Bahá replied: "The same crime for which Christ was indicted." The merchant was taken aback. He was a Christian, and here was a man speaking of similarity between His action and the action of Christ. "What could you know of Christ?" was his retort. 'Abdu'l-Bahá calmly proceeded to tell him. The arrogance of the merchant was confronted by the patience of 'Abdu'l-Bahá. When 'Abdu'l-Bahá rose to go, the merchant also rose and walked with Him into the street, betokening his respect for this Man – one of the detested prisoners. From then on, he was a friend, even more, a stout supporter.'[43] But regarding the charcoal, the merchant could only say, 'The coal is gone, – I cannot return you that, but here is the money.'[44]

37

Florence Khánum relates two sayings she heard from 'Abdu'l-Bahá. On one occasion He said to her ' "Ṣabr kun; mithl-i-Man básh" – be patient, be as I am. The other was when some one expressed discouragement to Him, saying they could not possibly acquire all the qualities and virtues that Bahá'ís are directed to possess, and the Master replied, "Kam Kam. Rúz bih rúz" – little by little; day by day.'[45]

38

As for Himself, 'Abdu'l-Bahá testified to His own patience as He eagerly waited for Bahá'ís to develop the spiritual virtues: 'Friends! The time is coming when I shall be no longer with you. I have done all that could be done. I have served the Cause of Bahá'u'lláh to the utmost of my ability. I have laboured night and day, all the years of my life. O how I long to see the loved ones taking upon themselves the responsibilities of the Cause!

Now is the time to proclaim the Kingdom of Bahá. Now is the hour of love and union! . . .

'Ah me, I am waiting, waiting, to hear the joyful tidings that the believers are the very embodiment of sincerity and truthfulness, the incarnation of love and amity, the living symbols of unity and concord. Will they not gladden my heart? Will they not satisfy my yearning? Will they not manifest my wish? Will they not fulfil my heart's desire? Will they not give ear to my call?

'I am waiting, I am patiently waiting.'[46]

39

Stanwood Cobb wrote that on one occasion He spoke of the need for loving patience in the face of aggravating behaviour on the part of others: 'One might say, "Well, I will endure such-and-such a person so long as he is endurable." *But Bahá'ís must endure people even when they are unendurable!*' Stanwood Cobb pointed out that 'He did not look at us solemnly as if appointing us to an arduous and difficult task. Rather, He beamed upon us delightfully, as if to suggest what a joy to us it would be to act in this way!'[47]

40

Professor Jakob Kunz and his wife, Anna, spoke with the Master in 1921. They wondered how one should deal with people who denied religion. He answered: 'You must be tolerant and patient, because the station of sight is a station of bounty; it is not based on capacity. They must be educated.'[48]

Fortitude

41

Bahá'u'lláh could trust 'Abdu'l-Bahá with the most difficult of tasks as He knew He would never waver. One such task was that of building a Shrine for the Báb on Mount Carmel, above what was then the small town of Haifa, facing the Mediterranean Sea. One of many obstacles which developed was that the owner of the plot, influenced by scheming Covenant-breakers, would not readily consent to sell the land. ' "Every stone of that building, every stone of the road leading to it," He, many a time was heard to remark, "I have with infinite tears and at tremendous cost, raised and placed in position." "One night," He, according to an eye-witness, once observed, "I was so hemmed in by My anxieties that I had no other recourse than to recite and repeat over and over again a prayer of the Báb which I had in My possession, the recital of which greatly calmed Me. The next morning the owner of the plot himself came to Me, apologized and begged Me to purchase his property." '[49]

42

A companion of 'Abdu'l-Bahá on His journey in America recorded a moment when the Master expressed His anxiety for the future: 'I am bearing these hardships of traveling so that the Cause of God may push on uncontaminated. For I am still anxious about what is going to happen after Me. Had I had ease of mind on this score I would have sat comfortably in one corner. I would not have come out of [the] Holy Land . . . I fear after Me self-seeking persons may disturb again the love

and unity of the friends.'[50] The Master talked in sorrowful tones until the automobile stopped at a hotel in
Chicago.

Integrity

43

Roy Wilhelm, an early pilgrim to the Master in 'Akká,
observed the esteem 'Abdu'l-Bahá had won from even
those who were not Bahá'ís: 'Our room fronted upon a
little garden in which was a fountain, and nearby a tent in
which 'Abdu'l-Bahá receives many of those who come to
see Him. So intense are the hatreds between the followers
of the different religious systems that it is unusual for a
man to be well spoken of outside his own system, but
'Abdu'l-Bahá is regarded by all classes as a man of such
wisdom and justice that it is to Him that they come for
explanation of their religious Books, for the adjustment
of their business quarrels, and even for the settlement of
family difficulties. The inquirer will be told that 'Abbás
Effendi ('Abdu'l-Bahá) makes no distinction; that He
helps Jew, Muḥammadan, and Christian alike.'[51] So fair
was He in His dealings that a just Governor of 'Akká,
Aḥmad Big Tawfíq, 'used to send his son to 'Abdu'l-
Bahá for instruction, and in the exercise of justice
and sound government turned to 'Abdu'l-Bahá for
counsel.'[52]

Sincerity

44

The Master once told a pilgrim the following story. He was concluding an interview by telling of the time when He was travelling with a party which included a merchant. When the caravan halted in a certain village, quite a few people gathered around to meet 'Abdu'l-Bahá. The travellers later continued their journey and when they stopped in another town the same thing happened, and then it happened again. The merchant noticed this very obvious love and respect, which were showered on the Master. He then took Him aside and told Him he wished to become a Bahá'í.

When the Master asked him why he desired this, he replied, without apparent shame, 'You are a Bahá'í, and wherever you go, great crowds of people flock out to meet you, while no one comes to meet me; so I wish to become a Bahá'í.' 'Abdu'l-Bahá probed deeper. He asked him if that was the real reason. Whereupon the merchant replied with candour, 'I also think it will help my business, as I will have all these people come to meet me.'

It was then that he was told very frankly, 'Do not become a Bahá'í. It is better for you to remain as you are.'[53]

Purity

45

The Master wrote to one lady as follows: 'Endeavor thou, as far as thou canst, in order that thou mayest be like unto a chaste and clear mirror, cleansed and purified from every dust, so that the outpouring of the rays of the Sun of Truth may descend and thou mayest illumine those who are around thee.'[54]

46

At the Fourth Annual Conference of the National Association for the Advancement of Colored People (NAACP), 'Abdu'l-Bahá asserted that 'every man imbued with divine qualities, who reflects heavenly moralities and perfections, who is the expression of ideal and praiseworthy attributes, is verily in the image and likeness of God . . . The character and purity of the heart is of all importance. The heart illumined by the light of God is nearest and dearest to God . . .'[55]

47

When 'Abdu'l-Bahá was asked at one time what He thought about women's fashions, He replied simply: 'We do not look upon the dresses of women, whether or not they are of the latest mode. We are not the judge of fashions. We rather judge the wearer of dresses. If she be chaste, if she be cultured, if she be characterized with heavenly morality, and if she be favored at the Threshold of God, she is honored and respected by us, no matter what manner of dress she wears. We have nothing to do with the ever-changing world of modes.'[56]

Chapter II

HIS KINDLY HEART

Let your heart burn with loving-kindness for all who may cross your path.[1]

'Abdu'l-Bahá

Kindliness

The above words of the Master during His visit to Paris were exemplified in His life, whether as a prisoner or a free man. As Shoghi Effendi, the Guardian of the Bahá'í Faith, wrote of Him, He was 'incomparable in the spontaneity, the genuineness and warmth of His sympathy and loving-kindness shown to friend and stranger alike, believer and unbeliever, rich and poor, high and low, whom He met, either intimately or casually, whether on board ship, or whilst pacing the streets, in parks or public squares, at receptions or banquets, in slums or mansions, in the gatherings of His followers or the assemblage of the learned, He, the incarnation of every Bahá'í virtue and the embodiment of every Bahá'í ideal . . .'[2] As one of His early admirers in the United States noted, 'He manifested what others mouthed.'[3]

I

One day, while 'Abdu'l-Bahá was in America, a young man named Fred Mortensen travelled all the way from Cleveland in the Midwest to Maine in the East in order to

33

see Him. Years later he wrote his own story. He was brought up in a very tough area and he belonged to a gang for which fighting, stealing and vandalism were a way of life. On one occasion he escaped from jail while awaiting trial and was a fugitive for four years. One day he tried to prevent a policeman from arresting another man and in the process was surprised by some detectives. He jumped off a thirty-five foot wall in an attempt to escape and broke his leg.

This brought him in touch with Albert Hall, a Bahá'í, who not only became his defender and helped him to gain his freedom, but also told him about the Bahá'í Faith. Although, at first, he found it bewildering, he was attracted and eventually his whole life changed. As he wrote: 'Thus the Word of God gave me a new birth . . .'

When 'Abdu'l-Bahá came to America in 1912 Fred Mortensen felt he was being urged by the Holy Spirit to make the journey to see Him. He had to attend a printers' convention in Cleveland but felt increasingly restless and decided to leave, come what may. He wrote: 'The night before leaving Cleveland I had a dream that I was 'Abdu'l-Bahá's guest, that I sat at a long table, and many others were there, too,˙ and of how he walked up and down telling stories, emphasizing with his hand. This, later, was fulfilled and he looked just as I saw him in Cleveland.

'As my finances were low I of necessity must hobo my way to Green Acre. The Nickel Plate Railway was my choice, for conveyance to Buffalo, New York. From Buffalo I again rode the rods to Boston, a long ride from around midnight until nine next morning. The Boston and Maine Railway was the last link between 'Abdu'l-Bahá and the outside world, so it seemed to me, and when I crawled off the top of one of its passenger trains at Portsmouth, New Hampshire, I was exceedingly happy.

A boat ride, a street car ride, and there I was, at the gate of Paradise. My heart beating double time, I stepped onto the soil of that to-be-famous center, tired, dirty, and wondering, but happy.'

He found that he was one of numerous people, all of whom wished also to see the beloved Master – and he was a very late arrival. Great was his astonishment the next day when he was told, ' 'Abdu'l-Bahá wishes to see Mr Mortensen.' It had seemed that the Master's first interview – with a doctor – had but begun. He was unprepared and 'nearly wilted'. He really somehow had expected to be called last.

Mr Mortensen recorded what happened next: 'He welcomed me with a smile and a warm hand-clasp, telling me to be seated, He sitting before me. His first words were, "Welcome! Welcome! You are very welcome," – then, "Are you happy?" – which was repeated three times.' Then came more queries, including one he had hoped to avoid: ' "Did you have a pleasant journey?"

'Of all the questions I wished to avoid this was the one! I dropped my gaze to the floor – and again he put the question. I lifted my eyes to his and his were as two black, sparkling jewels, which seemed to look into my very depths. I knew he knew and I must tell . . . I answered: "I did not come as people generally do, who come to see you."

'Question: "How did you come?"

'Answer: "Riding under and on top of the railway trains."

'Question: "Explain how."

'Now as I looked into the eyes of 'Abdu'l-Bahá I saw they had changed and a wondrous light seemed to pour out. It was the light of love and I felt relieved and very much happier. I explained to him how I rode on the trains, after which he kissed both my cheeks, gave me

35

much fruit, and kissed the dirty hat I wore, which had
become soiled on my trip to see him.'

When the Master prepared to leave Green Acre,
Mortensen was on hand to say farewell. Great indeed was
his astonishment when the Master requested him to
come into His car – he was thus blessed to be with
'Abdu'l-Bahá for a week in Malden, Massachusetts.
Finally he wrote: 'These events are engraved upon the
tablet of my heart and I love every moment of them. The
words of Bahá'u'lláh are my food, my drink and my life.
I have no other aim than to be of service in his pathway
and to be obedient to his Covenant.'[4]

2

A major event during the Master's visit to America was
the dedication of the land for the first Bahá'í House of
Worship of the western hemisphere in Wilmette, Illinois.
Mrs Nettie Tobin lived nearby in Chicago and was
anxious to contribute something, despite the fact that she
was not well off. The following is her account of how she
solved the problem. 'I had heard that the Master was to
be at the Temple site on May first, and I thought that He
should have a suitable stone to mark the location of the
Temple. So I went to a building under construction near
my home, and seeing a pile of stones at a wall, I asked the
builder if I could get a stone. He said, "Sure, help
yourself, these are rejected." So I went home, got an old,
small, baby carriage, loaded the stone into it and wheeled
it home. Early the next morning, with the help of a
Persian friend, I wheeled the carriage to the car line, and,
against the protests of the conductor, we got the carriage
onto the platform of the car. We made two changes and
finally, after endless delays, we got the baby carriage to
the corner of Central Street and Sheridan Road. Here,

when we pushed the carriage over a broken pavement it collapsed. As we stood despairing of getting the stone to the Temple grounds in time, since the hour had passed for the service, two boys with an express wagon came along. The boys were quickly persuaded to lend their wagon for the transportation and so we finally came to the grounds. Imagine my joy when "the stone refused by the builder" was received and used by the Master!'[5]

3

His kind heart went out to those who were ill. If He could alleviate a pain or discomfort, He set about to do so. We are told that one old couple who were ill in bed for a month had twenty visits from the Master during that time. In 'Akká, He daily sent a servant to inquire about the welfare of the ill, and as there was no hospital in the town, He paid a doctor a regular salary to look after the poor. The doctor was instructed not to tell Who provided this service. When a poor and crippled woman was shunned on contracting measles, the Master, on being informed, 'immediately engaged a woman to care for her; took a room, put comfortable bedding (His own) into it, called the doctor, sent food and everything she needed. He went to see that she had every attention, and when she died in peace and comfort, He it was Who arranged her simple funeral, paying all charges.'[6]

4

A man, ill with tuberculosis, was avoided by his friends – even his family was fearful and hardly dared enter his room. The Master needed only to hear of it and 'thereafter went daily to the sick man, took him delicacies, read and discoursed to him, and was alone with him when he died.'[7]

5

While in San Francisco, 'Abdu'l-Bahá visited a black believer, Mr Charles Tinsley, who had been confined to bed for a long time with a broken leg. The Master said to him: 'You must not be sad. This affliction will make you spiritually stronger. Do not be sad. Cheer up! Praise be to God, you are dear to me.'[8]

6

The Master delivered a short talk in New York City, which included the following: 'We should all visit the sick. When they are in sorrow and suffering it is a real help and benefit to have a friend come. Happiness is a great healer to those who are ill. In the East, it is the custom to call upon the patient often and meet him individually. The people in the East show the utmost kindness and compassion to the sick and suffering. This has greater effect than the remedy itself. You must always have this thought of love and affection when you visit the ailing and afflicted.'

Later 'Abdu'l-Bahá asserted, 'Bahá'u'lláh is the real Physician. He has diagnosed human conditions and indicated the necessary treatment. The essential principles of His healing remedies are the knowledge and love of God, severance from all else save God, turning our faces in sincerity toward the kingdom of God, implicit faith, firmness and fidelity, loving-kindness toward all creatures and the acquisition of the divine virtues indicated for the human world. These are the fundamental principles of progress, civilization, international peace and the unity of mankind. These are the essentials of Bahá'u'lláh's teachings, the secret of everlasting health, the remedy and healing for man.'[9]

Discipline

7

Kindness lies at the heart of loving discipline. 'Abdu'l-Bahá dearly loved His little grandson, Shoghi, but he needed to learn to be on time. This he learned very early in his life 'after receiving one good chastisement from no other hand than that of his grandfather!'[10] He then became the first to get up for the family prayers and breakfast.

Forgiveness

8

'Abdu'l-Bahá was born on the same night that the Báb declared His Mission in Shíráz on 22 May 1844, so on that day in 1906 it was about the Báb, His work and message, that He spoke. For the occasion over two hundred guests were to dine at the Master's table. Since dawn He had been busy helping with the work involved, Himself kneading dough to be put in the ovens, 'in gay spirits, inspiring, uplifting, cheering all His helpers'. Later He 'assisted in passing the platters . . . the rice . . . the lamb . . . the fruits of the region (of such large size, such colour, and such fragrance as only the sunshine of the East produces and paints). Moving among His two hundred guests, He spoke to them as He served them, such Divine words of love and spiritual import . . . "If one of you has been wounded in heart by the words or deeds of another, during the past year, forgive him now; that in purity of heart and loving pardon, you may feast in happiness, and arise, renewed in spirit." '[11]

9

It is related of Shaykh Maḥmúd of 'Akká that he 'hated the Bahá'ís. While many of his fellow-townsmen had gradually come to realize how very wrong they had been and were speaking of the prisoners in terms of appreciation and praise, Shaykh Maḥmúd remained adamant in his hatred. One day he was present at a gathering where people were talking of 'Abdu'l-Bahá as a good man, a remarkable man. The Shaykh could bear it no longer and stormed out, saying that he would show up this 'Abbás Effendi for what He was. In blazing anger he rushed to the mosque, where he knew 'Abdu'l-Bahá could be found at that hour, and laid violent hands upon Him. The Master looked at the Shaykh with that serenity and dignity which only He could command, and reminded him of what the Prophet Muḥammad had said: "Be generous to the guest, even should he be an infidel." Shaykh Maḥmúd turned away. His wrath had left him. So had his hate. All that he was conscious of was a deep sense of shame and bitter compunction. He fled to his house and barred the door. Some days later he went straight into the presence of 'Abdu'l-Bahá, fell on his knees, and besought forgiveness: "Which door but thine can I seek; whose bounty can I hope for but thine?" ' He became a devoted Bahá'í.[12]

10

In 1911 the Master spent a few quiet days in the French Alps, presumably to rest, before continuing to London. Here took place a remarkable encounter which illustrates the universality of His love, even towards those whose hearts ran hostile to Him and to His Father's Cause. Juliet Thompson tells us the following about this occasion which she herself witnessed: 'Monstrously sinned against, too great was He to claim the right to forgive. In His almost off-hand brushing aside of a cruelty, in the ineffable sweetness with which He ignored it, it was as though He said: Forgiveness belongs only to God.

'An example of this was His memorable meeting with the royal prince, Zillah Sulṭán, brother of the Sháh of Persia, Muḥammad 'Alí Sháh. Not alone 'Abdu'l-Bahá, but a great number of His followers, band after band of Bahá'í martyrs, had suffered worse than death at the hands of these two princes. When the downfall of the Sháh, with that of the Sulṭán of Turkey, set 'Abdu'l-Bahá at liberty, 'Abdu'l-Bahá, beginning His journey through Europe, went first to Thonon-les-Bains, on the Lake of Geneva. The exiled Sháh was then somewhere in Europe; Zillah-Sulṭán, also in exile with his two sons, had fled to Geneva. Thus 'Abdu'l-Bahá, the exonerated and free, and Zillah Sulṭán, the fugitive, were almost within a stone's throw of each other.

'In the suite of 'Abdu'l-Bahá was a distinguished European who had visited Persia and there met Zillah Sulṭán. One day when the European was standing on the balustraded terrace of the hotel in Thonon and 'Abdu'l-Bahá was pacing to and fro at a little distance, Zillah Sulṭán approached the terrace. 'Abdu'l-Bahá was wearing, as always, the turban, the long white belted robe and long 'abá of Persia. His hair, according to the ancient custom of the Persian nobility, flowed to His shoulders. Zillah Sulṭán, after greeting the European, immediately asked:

' "Who is that Persian nobleman?"

' " 'Abdu'l-Bahá."

' "Take me to Him."

'In describing the scene later, the European said: "If you could have heard the wretch mumbling his miserable excuses!" But 'Abdu'l-Bahá took the prince in His arms. "All that is of the past," He answered. "Never think of it again. Send your two sons to see me. I want to meet your sons."

'They came, one at a time. Each spent a day with the Master. The first, though an immature boy, nevertheless showed Him great deference. The second, older and more sensitive, left the room of 'Abdu'l-Bahá, where he had been received alone, weeping uncontrollably. "If only I could be born again," he said, "into any other family than mine."

'For not only had many Bahá'ís been martyred during his uncle's reign (upwards of a hundred by his father's instigation), and the life of 'Abdu'l-Bahá threatened again and again, but his grandfather, Náṣiri'd-Dín Sháh, had ordered the execution of the Báb, as well as the torture and death of thousands of Bábís.

'The young prince was "born again" – a Bahá'í.' [13]

II

Speaking to a group of friends at a meeting in Chicago in 1912, He said: 'Be in perfect unity. Never become angry with one another. Let your eyes be directed toward the kingdom of truth and not toward the world of creation. Love the creatures for the sake of God and not for themselves. You will never become angry or impatient if you love them for the sake of God. Humanity is not perfect. There are imperfections in every human being and you will always become unhappy if you look toward the people themselves. But if you look toward God you will love them and be kind to them, for the world of God is the world of perfection and complete mercy. Therefore do not look at the shortcomings of anybody; see with the sight of forgiveness.'[14]

Sensitivity

12

One day in London the hour for 'Abdu'l-Bahá's private audiences had arrived. Appointments had been made and, of necessity, an attempt was made to adhere to them rigidly. But 'Abdu'l-Bahá was a Man who taught moderation and consideration. A woman arrived without an appointment and was told it was not possible to fit her in, as 'Abdu'l-Bahá was talking with some 'most important people'. Descending the stairway, she was greatly disappointed. Suddenly, to her astonishment, a messenger from the Master dashed down to her saying that 'Abdu'l-Bahá wished to see her. With authority His voice was heard, saying: 'A heart has been hurt. Hasten, hasten, bring her to Me!'[15]

13

Two ladies from Scotland, delighted that their request to have an evening with the Master while He was in London had been granted, were warmly received by 'Abdu'l-

Bahá. How they relished having this intimate evening! Half an hour passed in His warm presence, when suddenly they were filled with consternation – an aggressive reporter strode into their midst and seated himself – he wanted information about the Master. His talkative, impolite manner left the ladies speechless – such an intrusion could spoil that precious evening.

Then, to their surprise, 'Abdu'l-Bahá stood up and, beckoning the reporter to follow Him, led the way into His room. The ladies had indeed got rid of the intruder, but they had also lost 'Abdu'l-Bahá. What were they to do?

Before long the hostess went to the Master's secretary and asked that He be informed 'that the ladies with whom the appointment had been made are awaiting His pleasure'.

Very soon kind words of farewell were heard. Then the Master returned, pausing by the door. Gravely, He looked at each and said, 'You were making that poor man uncomfortable, so strongly desiring his absence; I took him away to make him feel happy.'[16]

14

Maria Ioas longed to be the recipient of a flower from 'Abdu'l-Bahá. She had been tempted to ask pilgrims going to 'Akká to bring one to her, if at all possible. Yet, somehow, she felt she would receive one if the Master so desired. When He came to Chicago, she took one of her children and headed towards the Plaza Hotel on His first day there. He was away, so they waited the entire afternoon. As He stepped out of the elevator, He saw them and greeted them kindly. He then headed for His room and bade them follow. She hesitated and He again urged, 'Come, come.' Then they felt free to accompany

Him into His reception room. Shortly after, He emerged from His private room carrying roses and graciously handed one to her.[17]

15

When 'Abdu'l-Bahá was in San Francisco, His hostess arranged an interview with the Mayor of Berkeley. Many dignitaries and university people were to gather at a reception.

'As the appointed hour for departure approached the hostess went upstairs to warn Abdul-Baha that the time was near. He smiled and waved her away, saying "Very soon! Very soon!"

'She left him with some impatience, for there was no evidence of preparation for the trip. After some time she went up again, for the automobile was honking at the door, and it looked as if the Mayor of Berkeley would be kept waiting. But she met only a smile, and "Very soon! Very soon!" from the important guest. At last her patience was quite exhausted for she knew that they could not possibly arrive at the reception in time. Suddenly there was a ring at the door bell. Immediately Abdul-Baha's step was on the stair, and when the door opened he was beside the maid, pulling over the threshold a dusty and disheveled man whom no one had ever heard of, but whom Abdul-Baha embraced like a long lost friend.' He had read of 'Abdu'l-Bahá in the newspapers and felt he must see Him, but as he did not have enough money for the car fare, he walked the fifteen miles into San Francisco. Had 'Abdu'l-Bahá left on time, they would have missed each other – but the Master had 'felt his approach' and would not leave until His guest was seated at the table with tea and sandwiches. Only then could the Master say, 'Now I must go, but when you have finished, wait for Me in My room upstairs, until I return, and then we will have a great talk.'[18]

16

In London it was noted that inquirers often hated to leave. If any were still present when luncheon or dinner was to be served, they were inevitably invited to dine also. To smother embarrassment, 'Abdu'l-Bahá would extend His hand to the humblest and lead him personally into the dining-room, seating him at His right and talking with such warmth that soon the surprised guest felt completely at ease. As many as eighteen might find themselves being served by the Master Himself, but He was prone to continue His interrupted conversations or to tell an anecdote, often sparkling with His humour.[19]

17

Bahá'u'lláh wrote: 'The wise are they that speak not unless they obtain a hearing, even as the cup-bearer, who proffereth not his cup till he findeth a seeker . . .'[20] A delightful story is told of a Mademoiselle Letitia, who had come from a poor family in Haifa to live in the Master's home in 'Akká to teach French to the children. She was happy there, though she was a Catholic and the nuns in the convent watched over her. One day, when a French pilgrim came for a visit, her services as translator were needed, as no one else knew French. Mademoiselle became embarrassed and later confessed to the nuns. For a number of days thereafter she looked very stern. 'Abdu'l-Bahá, noticing this, called her to Him and reassured her: 'Letitia, tell the good nuns that they need have no fear. I asked you to interpret for me because there was no one else to speak French, not because I desired to teach you. We have so many Bahais, who come here, begging with all their hearts and all their love for instruction, that only to them do we give our precious teaching.

'You would have to beg and beg and *beg* before I would give it to you, and even then I might not do so; for it is not so cheap as to be bestowed where it is not wanted.

'Stay in the home if you like, or go if you are not happy here. We are glad to have you if you care to stay, but free your heart of all fear that we will try to make a Bahai of you.'[21]

Encouragement

18

In Paris on one occasion a man from India stated frankly to 'Abdu'l-Bahá: 'My aim in life is to transmit as far as in me lies the message of Krishna to the world.'

In His loving way the Master replied: 'The Message of Krishna is the message of love. All God's prophets have brought the message of love. None has ever thought that war and hate are good. Every one agrees in saying that love and kindness are best.'[22]

A negative approach would have hurt this man. The Master did not offer argument. Instead He showed appreciation, and thus He encouraged this devout follower of Krishna.

19

When 'Abdu'l-Bahá was in London, there was a work-man who had left his bag of tools in a hall. He chanced upon the smiling Master. Sadly the workman told of his predicament: 'I don't know much about religious things, as I have no time for anything but my work.'

Words of reassurance came in reply: 'That is well. Very well. A day's work done in the spirit of service is in itself an act of worship. Such work is a prayer unto God.'[23]

20

When the Master was on the steamship *Celtic*, a woman came to Him with her problem: she was afraid of death. He said to her: 'Then do something that will keep you from dying; that will instead, day by day make you more alive, and bring you everlasting life. According to the words of His Holiness Christ, those who enter the Kingdom of God will never die. Then enter the Divine Kingdom, and fear death no more.'

They spoke of the Atlantic Ocean – it was temporarily quiet. He advised: 'One must ride in the Ship of God; for this life is a stormy sea, and all the people on earth – that is, over two billion souls – will drown in it before a hundred years have passed. All, except those who ride in the Ship of God. Those will be saved.'[24]

'Abdu'l-Bahá and visitors at the Clifton Guest House in Bristol,
England, September, 1911

'Abdu'l-Bahá with a child outside His home in
Haifa, July, 1921

21

The Master made it quite clear that people of very different capacities were qualified to teach this great Faith, each in his own way. John David Bosch, who had come to America from Switzerland, felt that he could not be a speaker – instead he circulated pamphlets and books. The Master encouraged him: 'You are doing very well; you are doing better than talking. With you it is not words or the movement of the lips; with you it is the heart that speaks. In your presence silence speaks and radiates.'[25]

22

Juliet Thompson, a devout Bahá'í and a New York artist, was told by 'Abdu'l-Bahá that she taught well. Frankly and lovingly, He said to her: 'I have met many people who have been affected by you, Juliet. You are not eloquent; you are not fluent, but your *heart* teaches. You speak with an emotion – a feeling which makes people ask, "What is this that she has?"'[26]

23

In 1919, when Margaret Randall, who came to be known as Bahíyyih, was but thirteen years of age, she went to Haifa with her parents and others to see 'Abdu'l-Bahá. Bahíyyih has recounted some of her experiences: 'One night we were sitting at the table with 'Abdu'l-Bahá. He always placed me on His left. He smiled at me and said, "Your name is Bahíyyih. Bahíyyih means light, but unless you have something within you, something back of it, there is no light." And I realized the challenge He gave me just then. Another time we were told that we could have an interview with 'Abdu'l-Bahá and mother went with me when I had one. I asked Him, "What can I do to serve this Faith?" The Master paced up and down the room . . . "Study. Study. Study." So many times the Master would repeat things three times. That was the message for me. Always the Master knew the thing that would bring fullest development into the individual's life. If it was requested, He guided the person to it.'[27]

Gentleness

24

After Bahá'u'lláh's confinement in the Most Great Prison in 'Akká had ended, but while He was yet residing in the town, an Egyptian merchant, 'Abdu'l-Karím, afire with God's latest message, desired to visit Him. He wrote for permission to go on pilgrimage. He must have been greatly surprised when the reply arrived: he might go on pilgrimage but only after all his debts were paid.

He had been in business for many years. His caravans crossed the desert with precious cargo. He had quite naturally been interested in expanding his business, but now his consuming interest was to 'owe no man anything'. It followed that when he received a payment, instead of investing it for further gain, he paid off a debt. This continued for five years, until at last he was debt-free.

His business shrank. No longer did 'love of wealth' consume him. When all his debts were paid, he had only enough to keep his family going in his absence and to pay for deck passage on a ship bound for Haifa.

Formerly, he would have travelled first-class. Now he had neither bed nor warm stateroom. Never mind! He was going to see Bahá'u'lláh. As he crossed the gang-plank, his shawl slipped into the water. The night would be chilly, but his heart was glad and he felt 'alive with prayer'.

Bahá'u'lláh informed His family that He was expecting an honoured guest. A carriage was sent to Haifa to pick up the merchant, but the attendant received no description of this very special guest. As the passengers disembarked, he watched them very carefully – surely he would recognize someone so distinguished – but the passengers appeared quite ordinary and in due time he returned to 'Akká with word that Bahá'u'lláh's visitor had not arrived.

The merchant had expected to be met. He had no money left to hire a carriage. Bitterly disappointed, he seated himself on a bench, feeling forlorn and destitute.

Bahá'u'lláh knew that His distinguished guest had arrived, even though he had not been recognized. This time He sent 'Abdu'l-Bahá, who, in the twilight, recognized 'the disappointed figure huddled upon the bench'. Quickly the Master introduced Himself and explained what had happened. Then He asked the traveller if he would like to go to 'Akká that very night or if he would prefer to wait until morning. The merchant had already spent hours in prayer in preparation for his meeting with Bahá'u'lláh, but now he found that bitterness had seeped into his heart – he had felt so forgotten and alone upon his arrival in Haifa. He had even begun to wonder about the very station of Bahá'u'lláh. For what had he given up his fortune? He was in spiritual torment. However, in the presence of this welcome and gentle Man, doubts and suspicions ebbed out of his soul; yet he felt the need of hours of prayer to feel spiritually ready to meet God's Emissary.

As the story is told, 'Abbás Effendi knew instinctively that His new friend would not wish to seek a hotel at His expense, so finding that he preferred to wait until morning for the journey to 'Akká, 'he unbuttoned the long cloak that enveloped him, seated himself beside the pilgrim, and wrapped both in its ample folds. So they passed the night praying together, lost in that ecstasy of prayer that brings realization.'

The next morning they proceeded towards the prison-city of 'Akká. At long last the Egyptian appeared before Bahá'u'lláh with a glad heart, purified through five years of testing.[28]

25

May Bolles (Maxwell) was one of fifteen fortunate pilgrims welcomed in the prison-city from December 1898 to early 1899. She recorded her experiences in *An Early Pilgrimage* – a divine love story!

In the Holy Land, whose very air was 'laden with the perfume of roses and orange blossoms', she found 'Abdu'l-Bahá whose love, wisdom and gentleness penetrated her very soul. In 'Akká the Holy Family had vacated their own rooms that the pilgrims might be comfortable. Early each morning the Master would inquire about their happiness and health, and at night He would wish them 'beautiful dreams' and a good rest. There, for three precious days and nights, they heard nothing 'but the mention of God'. Never, elsewhere, had she seen such happiness, or heard so much laughter. The Master wanted no tears. At one time He asked some pilgrims who were moved to tears to weep no more for

His sake. Only when all were fully composed would He teach the friends.

She wrote, 'We had learned that to be with 'Abdu'l-Bahá was all life, joy and blessedness. We were to learn also that His Presence is a purifying fire. The pilgrimage to the Holy City is naught but a crucible in which the souls are tried; where the gold is purified and the dross is consumed. It did not seem possible that anything but love could ever again animate our words and actions. Yet that very afternoon, in my room with two of the believers, I spoke against a brother in the truth, finding fault with him, and giving vent to the evil in my own heart by my words. While we were still sitting together, our Master, who had been visiting the poor and sick, returned, and immediately sent for my spiritual mother, Lua, who was with us. He told her that during His absence one of His servants had spoken unkindly of another, and that it grieved His heart that the believers should not love one another or that they should speak against any soul. Then He charged her not to speak of it but to pray. A little later we all went to supper, and my hard heart was unconscious of its error, until, as my eyes sought the beloved face of my Master, I met His gaze, so full of gentleness and compassion that I was smitten to the heart. For in some marvellous way His eyes spoke to me; in that pure and perfect mirror I saw my wretched self and burst into tears. He took no notice of me for a while and everyone kindly continued with the supper while I sat in His dear Presence washing away some of my sins in tears. After a few moments He turned and smiled on me and spoke my name several times as though He were calling me to Him. In an instant such sweet happiness pervaded my soul, my heart was comforted with such infinite hope, that I knew He would cleanse me of all my sins.'[29]

26

One day 'Abdu'l-Bahá, an interpreter, and Howard Colby Ives, at that time a Unitarian minister, were alone in a reception room. Colby Ives later wrote: ' 'Abdu'l-Bahá had been speaking of some Christian doctrine and His interpretation of the words of Christ was so different from the accepted one that I could not restrain an expression of remonstrance. I remember speaking with some heat: "How is it possible to be so sure?" I asked. "No one can say with certainty what Jesus meant after all these centuries of misinterpretation and strife."

'He intimated that it was quite possible.

'It is indicative of my spiritual turmoil and my blindness to His station, that instead of His serenity and tone of authority impressing me as warranted it drove me to actual impatience. "That I cannot believe," I exclaimed.

'I shall never forget the glance of outraged dignity the interpreter cast upon me. It was as though he would say: "Who are you to contradict or even to question 'Abdu'l-Bahá!"

'But not so did 'Abdu'l-Bahá look at me. How I thank God that it was not! He looked at me a long moment before He spoke. His calm, beautiful eyes searched my soul with such love and understanding that all my momentary heat evaporated. He smiled as winningly as a lover smiles upon his beloved, and the arms of His spirit seemed to embrace me as He said softly that I should try my way and He would try His.'[30]

Sympathy and Understanding

'Abdu'l-Bahá's deep sympathy and understanding for the human condition, with its frailties and needs, generated His natural desire to help as much as was possible.

27

In 'Akká the Master's room often contained not even a bed as He was continually giving His own to those more needy than He. Wrapped in a blanket, He would lie on the floor or even on the roof of His home. It was not possible to buy a bed in the town of 'Akká; a bed ordered from Haifa took at least thirty-six hours to arrive. Inevitably, when the Master went on His morning round of visitations and found a feverish individual tossing on bare ground, He sent him His bed. Only after His own situation was inadvertently discovered did He receive another bed, thanks to some kind friend.[31]

28

During His last earthly hours 'Abdu'l-Bahá lay in bed with a fever and His night-robe needed changing. However, none could be found, as He had given them away.[32]

29

When a Turkish man, living in Haifa, lost his position, he, his wife and children were in desperate need. They went to 'Abdu'l-Bahá for help and were naturally greatly aided. When the poor man became ill, again the Master stood ready to help. He provided a doctor, medicine and provisions to make him comfortable. When this man felt he was to die, he asked for 'Abdu'l-Bahá and called his children to him. 'Here', he told the children, 'is your father, who will take care of you when I am gone.'

One morning four small children arrived at the home of 'Abdu'l-Bahá and announced, 'We want our father.' The Master, hearing their voices, knew who they were. They shared their sorrow with Him – their own father had died.

'Abdu'l-Bahá brought them in and gave them drink, sweets and cakes. He then went with them to their home. Their announcement had been premature – their father had merely fainted, but the next day he passed away.

The Master arranged for the funeral and provided food, clothing and travel-tickets for the family to go to Turkey. His sympathetic heart was as wide as the universe.[33]

30

'When He reached the Occident, however, 'Abdu'l-Bahá faced a condition which troubled Him greatly, because it was beyond His power to assuage the misery He saw constantly about Him. Housed luxuriously at Cadogan Gardens, London, He knew that within a stone's throw of Him were people who had never had enough to eat – and in New York there was exactly the same situation. These things made Him exceedingly sad, and He said: "The time will come in the near future when humanity will become so much more sensitive than at present that the man of great wealth will not enjoy his luxury, in comparison with the deplorable poverty about him. He will be forced, for his own happiness, to expend his wealth to procure better conditions for the community in which he lives." '34

31

So sensitive and sympathetic was the Master to human suffering that He admitted to surprise that others could be quite oblivious to it. In Paris, He expressed His feelings: 'I have just been told that there has been a terrible accident in this country. A train has fallen into the river and at least twenty people have been killed. This is going to be a matter for discussion in the French Parliament today, and the Director of the State Railway will be called upon to speak. He will be cross-examined as to the condition of the railroad and as to what caused the accident, and there will be a heated argument. I am filled with wonder and surprise to notice what interest and excitement has been aroused throughout the whole country on account of the death of twenty people, while they remain cold and indifferent to the fact that thousands of Italians, Turks, and Arabs are killed in Tripoli! The horror of this wholesale slaughter has not disturbed the Government at all! Yet these unfortunate people are human beings too.'35

Generosity

'Abdu'l-Bahá gave freely of what He had – love, time, care and concern, food and money, clothing and flowers, a bed, a rug! His motto appeared to be: frugality for Himself, generosity for others.

Stories of the Master's self-denial in favour of others' well-being are legion. He was 'bountiful as the rain in His generosity to the poor . . .'[36] Because He and His family were rich in the love of God, they accepted material deprivation for themselves gladly. On the other hand, if the Master knew of a broken window or a leaky roof, which were health hazards, He would make sure the necessary repairs were completed.[37]

He did not need, or want, luxury. This became obvious on His trip to America. Once, after a few days in beautiful rooms reserved for Him by the friends in one city, He moved to a simple apartment. However, in hotels He tipped so generously as to cause astonishment. In homes where He was entertained, He left thoughtful gifts for both hosts and servants. It should be emphasized that He went from coast to coast to speak without pay or benefit of contract.

32

'Abdu'l-Bahá's generosity was natural to Him already in childhood. A story is recorded of the time when young 'Abbás Effendi went to the mountains to see the thousands of sheep which His Father then owned. The shepherds, wishing to honour their young Guest, gave Him a feast. Before 'Abbás was taken home at the close of the day, the head shepherd advised Him that it was customary under the circumstances to leave a present for the shepherds. 'Abbás told the man that He had nothing to give. Yet the shepherd persisted that He must give something. Whereupon the Master gave them all the sheep.

We are told that when Bahá'u'lláh heard about this incident, He laughed and commented, 'We will have to protect 'Abdu'l-Bahá from Himself – some day he will give himself away.'[38]

33

It is told that in the home of Bahá'u'lláh there was a beautiful rug upon which He used to sit. One day a poor Arab brought a load of wood to the house. He saw the rug and was very much attracted by its beauty. He handled it with great appreciation and exclaimed, 'Oh, how wonderful it must be to have such a splendid rug to sit upon!'

'Abdu'l-Bahá heard him and said, 'If you like the rug, take it.'

The man could not believe it was really a gift. Fearing he would lose it, he put it over his shoulder and began to run, looking back to see if anyone was coming to take it from him.

With delicious humour 'Abdu'l-Bahá said, 'Go on, no one is going to take it away from you.'[39]

34

Another instance of His generosity concerned a rug, which was among 'the most exquisite' ever created in Persia. Woven of 'purest silk, patterned as a rose garden and bordered with heavy twisted cord of real gold', it was bought from merchants after World War I. With great effort it was brought to Haifa by way of Afghánistán and India, due to transportation and travel problems.

When the generous pilgrim arrived after tiring weeks of travel, he took the rug to the Pilgrim House adjacent to the Shrine of the Báb and spread it out on the floor. 'Abdu'l-Bahá arrived and 'immediately inquired of the caretaker whose carpet that was, and upon being told, He said that so valuable a work of art should not be on the

floor where it might become soiled and He gave instructions for it to be rolled up and put away. The pilgrim then
told 'Abdu'l-Bahá that the carpet had been brought for
Him and He replied that so beautiful a gift should be
placed in the Shrine of Bahá'u'lláh, and that He would
place it there Himself.'

Within a few days resident believers and pilgrims went
with 'Abdu'l-Bahá to Bahjí. They boarded a train in
Haifa for 'Akká. From 'Akká a carriage took the older
friends to Bahjí. The Master rode His now-famous white
donkey, the younger ones walked.

The pilgrim from the East 'offered the Master some
chocolate and this He shared with some others.' He
related that 'we asked permission of the Master to sing
and when He graciously permitted us, we began to sing. I
do not remember what the songs were, whether they
were our chants or other songs, but I know that I never
felt so happy in my life as then when singing in the
presence of the Master, and I am sure all the others felt the
same way. After we reached Bahjí we had dinner and
then 'Abdu'l-Bahá spread the carpet in the Holy Shrine,
and thus my hope was realized.'*[40]

35

'Abdu'l-Bahá was invited to speak before the Eighteenth
Annual Lake Mohonk Conference on International
Arbitration held at Mohonk Mountain House, a beauti-
ful mountain-top resort on a small, forest-fringed,
jewel-like lake – Mohonk Lake – in southern New York.
Many influential people attended these conferences.

He ended His talk by saying, 'It is the Holy Spirit of

* This exquisite rug – 'the most valuable ornament of Bahá'u'lláh's Shrine' –
was eventually donated by Shoghi Effendi to the Bahá'í House of Worship
in Wilmette, Illinois.

God which insures the safety of humanity, for human thoughts differ, human susceptibilities differ. You cannot make the susceptibilities of all humanity one except through the common channel of the Holy Spirit.'[41] He was heartily applauded, but was too tired to continue speaking.

The day before He was to leave, 'Abdu'l-Bahá decided He would like to present the president of the Conference with a choice Persian rug which was, unfortunately, in His flat in New York. Dr Díyá Baghdádí performed the seemingly impossible task of fetching the rug all that distance in one night and arrived just as 'Abdu'l-Bahá was 'shaking hands with Mr Smiley', preparing to leave. Albert Smiley must have been astonished for he said, 'Why, this is just what I have been seeking for many years! You see, we had a Persian rug just like this one, but it was burned in a fire and ever since my wife has been broken-hearted over it. This will surely make her very happy.'[42] As far as the author is aware, the rug is still in use in Mountain House.

36

'Abdu'l-Bahá would refuse generous sums of money meant for Himself but would accept a small token of love, such as a handkerchief. In London a lady said to the Master, 'I have here a cheque from a friend, who begs its acceptance to buy a good motor-car for your work in England and Europe.' To this 'Abdu'l-Bahá replied, 'I accept with grateful thanks the gift of your friend.' He took the cheque into both His hands, as though blessing it, and said, 'I return it to be used for gifts to the poor.'[43]

On another occasion an American lady wished to donate money to the Master '. . . for his own use or for that of the Cause. He replied that he could not himself accept a gift from her; but that if she wished to do something for him, she should educate the two little girls of a Christian schoolmaster in Haifa, who had recently lost his wife, was very poor, and in much trouble. She accordingly sent these children to a school in Beyrout.'[44]

The Bahá'ís in America desired to contribute $18,000 for the Master's projected trip to their shores. When the funds began to reach the Master, He returned them, asking that they donate the money instead to charity.

37

'When 'Abdu'l-Bahá first arrived in England, he was the guest of a friend in a village not far from London. The evident poverty around him in this wealthy country distressed him greatly. He would walk out in the town, garbed in his white turban and long Persian coat, and all eyes were centered upon this strange visitor, who, the people had been told, was "a holy man from the East". Naturally the children were attracted to him, followed him, pulled at his coat, or his hand, and were immediately taken into his arms and caressed. This delighted them, of course, and children are never afraid of 'Abdu'l-Bahá, but what pleased and amazed them still more was that when they were put down, they found in their little hands a shilling or sixpence from the capacious pockets of "the holy Man's" long coat. Such bits of silver were a rarity in their experience, and they ran home with joy to tell the tale of the generous stranger from the Orient, possessed apparently of an endless store of shining sixpences.

'The children crowded after him and so many six-pences were dispensed that the friend who entertained 'Abdu'l-Bahá became alarmed, and talked the matter over with Miss Robarts, who was also a guest in the house. "It is a shame!" they said indignantly. "He comes to us accepting nothing, and is giving to our people all the time! It must not go on!"

'That day 'Abdu'l-Bahá had bestowed many sixpences, and people had come from the neighboring villages, bringing their children to receive the blessing from "the holy Man" – and of course the sixpences! About nine o'clock in the evening the ladies decided that no one else must see 'Abdu'l-Bahá that night. But as they waited outside the cottage, a man came up the path, carrying one baby, and with others clinging to him. When he asked for "the holy Man", however, he was told severely that he could not be seen, he was very tired and had gone to bed. The man sighed, as he said, "Oh, I have walked six miles from far away to see Him. I am so sorry!"

'The hostess responded severely, feeling that the desire for sixpences had prompted the journey perhaps more than religious enthusiasm, and the man sighed more deeply than ever, and was turning away, when suddenly 'Abdu'l-Bahá came around the corner of the house. The way in which he embraced the man and all the babies was so wonderful, that the hearts of the too careful friends melted within them, and when he at last sent away the unbidden guests, comforted, their hearts full of joy, their hands bursting with sixpences, the two friends looked at one another and said: "How wrong we were! We will never again try to manage 'Abdu'l-Bahá!" '[45]

38

For 'Abdu'l-Bahá inexpensive clothes were sufficient. One day He was to entertain the Governor of 'Akká. His wife felt that His coat was hardly worthy of the occasion. Well ahead of time she went to the tailor where she ordered a fine coat, thinking that, with His lack of self-consciousness, He would surely not notice that His old coat was missing. He desired, after all, only to be scrupulously clean. The new garment was laid out at the proper time, but the Master went searching for His own coat. He asked for it, insisting that the one laid out was not His. His wife attempted to explain the new coat, but He would have none of it, and He told her why: 'But think of this! . . . For the price of this coat you can buy five such as I ordinarily use, and do you think I would spend so much money upon a coat which only I shall wear? If you think I need a new one, very well, but send this back and have the tailor make Me for this price five such as I usually have. Then you see, I shall not only have a new one, but I shall also have four to give to others!'[46]

39

Cloak and coat stories pertaining to 'Abdu'l-Bahá are numerous. Once, before the Master's wife went on a journey, she left a second cloak for 'Abdu'l-Bahá with one of their daughters, for she feared He would give His away and be caught without one in her absence. The daughter was not to tell her Father about the second cloak, but amazingly, the Master soon asked His daughter if He had another cloak, so the truth had to be told. As was to be expected, He replied, 'How could I be happy having two cloaks, knowing that there are those that have none?' He gave the second one away.[47]

40

At one time the Master had a fine cloak of Persian wool, which had been given to Him. When a poor man appealed to Him for a garment, He sent for this cloak and gave it to him. The man took it but complained, saying it was only of cotton.

'No,' 'Abbás Effendi assured him, 'it is of wool'; and to prove it He lighted a match and burned a little of the nap. The man still grumbled that it was not good. 'Abbás Effendi reproved him for criticizing a gift, but He ended the interview by directing an attendant to give the man a mejidi (a coin then worth about four francs). It was observed that if someone vexed the Master, He always gave him a gift.[48]

41

Major Wellesley Tudor-Pole wrote in his diary in 1918, at the time of his visit to the Master, 'I gave him the Persian camel-hair cloak, and it greatly pleased him, for the winter is here, and he had given away the only cloak he possessed. I made him promise to keep this one through the winter anyway, and I trust he does.'[49]

42

Before a winter's cold took hold of 'Akká, the Master would go to a clothing shop where He would arrange that a number of the poor should come to receive their annual cloaks. He would adjust the garments over some of those poor shoulders. He gave where He felt it was merited and kept a record of the recipients. He did not wish to be abused – but even abuse was known to receive kindness at His generous hands, as has been shown.[50] Small wonder that the Arabs called Him the 'Lord of Generosity'[51] and Bahá'ís became ablaze by observing His actions of continuing kindness and loved Him as the Servant of God.

43

Mary Lucas, a pilgrim to 'Akká in 1905, found that the Master gave away all the many gifts which were sent to Him. 'A story is told of a beautiful silver service which was presented to Him, and He did not even look at it. One and another received portions of it until piece by piece it disappeared.

'A significant incident is that of a wealthy woman who offered Him a sum of money before she left 'Akká. He refused to accept it, and as the lady pleaded for the privilege of placing it in His hands, He said, at length: "I never accept anything for Myself, but if you wish you may bestow it upon a poor man . . . for the education of his son." So the money was used for this purpose.'[52]

Charity

Already in 'Abdu'l-Bahá's day relief funds had been established. He encouraged the Save the Children Fund. The Haifa Relief Fund had been created to alleviate the misery of the local population – twice the Master contributed fifty Egyptian pounds. After the first contribution His name was placed first on the contributors' list. After receiving the second, the Military Governor, G. A. Stanton, wrote a letter of gratitude in which he stated, 'Please accept on behalf of the committee of management, my very sincerest and most grateful thanks for this further proof of your well-known generosity and care of the poor, who will forever bless you for your liberality on their behalf.'[53]

44

Among the most touching contacts the Master had with the poor in the Occident were surely His visits to the Salvation Army headquarters in London and to the Bowery Mission in New York City.

'On Christmas night, 1912, 'Abdu'l-Bahá visited a Salvation Army Shelter in London where a thousand homeless men ate a special Christmas dinner. He spoke to them while they ate, reminding them that Jesus had been poor and that it was easier for the poor than the rich to enter the Kingdom of Heaven. The men sat enthralled. Some were so impressed that in spite of hunger and the special dinner before them they forgot to eat. When, on leaving, 'Abdu'l-Bahá gave the warden of the Shelter money with which to buy a similar dinner on New Year's night, the men rose to their feet to cheer Him as He went, waving their knives and forks in the air. They little realised that He had experienced trials, hardship and suffering far greater than any they had known.'[54]

Before 'Abdu'l-Bahá went to the Bowery Mission, He asked friends to convert a thousand-franc note into quarters. At the Mission, in April 1912, He spoke most lovingly to the several hundred men who were present: 'You must be thankful to God that you are poor, for His Holiness Jesus Christ has said "Blessed are the poor"; He never said Blessed are the rich. He said too that the kingdom is for the poor and that it is easier for a camel to enter a needle's eye than for a rich man to enter God's kingdom.' And then He told them, 'When Jesus Christ appeared it was the poor who first accepted Him, not the rich.' And later, 'The rich are mostly negligent, inattentive, steeped in worldliness, depending upon their means whereas the poor are dependent upon God and their reliance is upon Him, not upon themselves. Therefore the poor are nearer the threshold of God and His throne.'[55]

He closed with characteristic humbleness, asking the men to accept Him as their servant. After the talk, He stood at the Mission Hall entrance. He took each hand and placed in each a number of coins – the price of a bed for the night. However, at least one man kept his money, explaining, 'That was a heavenly man, and his quarter was not like other quarters, it will bring me luck!'[56] But some eighty quarters remained. When the Master arrived at His apartment building, He encountered the chambermaid who had previously been the happy recipient of His roses. Now He emptied all the remaining quarters into her apron. He quickly moved on. When she learned of His gifts at the Mission, she vowed she also would give this money away. Juliet Thompson recalled, 'Later, as we sat in a group around the Master, who was at that moment saying with a laugh (in reply to some question as to the advisability of charity), "Assuredly, give to the poor! If you give them only words, when they put their hands into their pockets they will find themselves none the richer for you!" There came a light tap at the door and there on the threshold stood the little chambermaid. Her eyes were glistening with tears and in a sort of wonder, and oblivious of the rest of us, she walked straight up to the Master:

' "I came to say good-bye, sir," she said, timidly and brokenly, "and to thank you for all your goodness to me . . . I never expected such goodness. And to ask you – to *pray* for me!"

'Her head drooped, her voice broke . . . she turned and went out quickly.'[57]

'Abdu'l-Bahá with children in New York

'Abdu'l-Bahá entering the garden of His house in Haifa,
November, 1921

45

In 1907 Corinne True was in 'Akká with the Master. She was one of many who were deeply touched by the love of 'Abdu'l-Bahá, demonstrated so clearly in His customary Friday morning acts of charity. From her window she 'saw between two and three hundred men, women and children gathered. Such a motley crowd one can see only in these parts. There were blind, lame, cripples and very feeble persons, the poorest clad collection of people almost that the earth contains. One man had his clothing made of a patched quilt, an old woman had gunny sacking for a cloak; children were so ragged that their clothing would scarcely stay on them.

'Two or three of the men believers were with the Master. The people were required to arrange themselves in order about two sides of the court and the Master began near the gate giving into the hand of each some piece of money and then each was required to move out. It was a sight never to be forgotten to see the Master going from one to another, saying some word of praise or kindness to encourage each. With some He would stop to inquire into their health and He would pat them on the back, these poor, dirty-looking creatures, and once in a while we would see Him send some one away empty-handed and He would reprimand him for his laziness. How clear and musical His voice sounded as He went from one to another, giving and praising! The men accompanying Him kept order in great kindness, but firmness, and saw that each passed on as soon as he had received from the Master. Where on this globe can one duplicate such a scene as is enacted every Friday morning in the court yard of the Master of Acca, Who is Himself a state Prisoner to the Turkish government and has lived in prison or in exile since He was nine years of age!'[58]

Later, while resting, the Master told Mrs True about His friends. 'These are My friends, *My* friends. Some of them are My enemies, but they think I do not know it, because they appear friendly, and to them I am very kind, for one must love his enemies and do good to them.' He explained that there simply was not sufficient work in 'Akká. Men could do but two kinds of work: they could fish, but the sea had been too stormy lately, or they could carry loads on their backs, which required great strength. Those who attempted to deceive Him were rebuked and told where they might obtain work.[59]

46

'Roy', another early pilgrim, described what he saw: 'Friday mornings at seven there is another picture. Near the tent in the garden one may see an assemblage of the abject poor – the lame, the halt and the blind – seldom less than a hundred. As 'Abdu'l-Bahá passes among them He will be seen to give to each a small coin, and to add a word of sympathy or cheer; often an inquiry about those at home; frequently He sends a share to an absent one. It is a sorry procession as they file slowly away, but they all look forward to this weekly visit, and indeed it is said that this is the chief means of sustenance for some of them. Almost any morning, early, He may be seen making the round of the city, calling upon the feeble and the sick; many dingy abodes are brightened by His presence.'[60]

Sacrifice

How could this Prisoner give to the needy of 'Akká every Friday morning? Had not His exiled family's wealth and property been almost totally confiscated? One pilgrim found that, 'All that the Master gives is a real sacrifice, and is saved by the cutting off of what most people would consider necessities.'[61]

What most impressed 'Roy' was the spirit of sacrifice which he found among the Bahá'ís in the 'Most Great Prison'. He noted that, 'Nowhere have I witnessed such love, such perfect harmony. The desire of those in that prison was to serve one another.'[62]

The Master spoke to him in Persian with an interpreter. After saying that 'The Cause of God is like a tree – its fruit is love', He asked how the believers were. Happy that they were becoming more united He replied, 'This news is the cause of My happiness, for the more they are united the more they will receive God's confirmation. They must love one another. Each must devote and sacrifice himself and what he has for the other. I, Myself, sacrifice My life for all.'[63]

47

'Abdu'l-Bahá knew how to give – not just what He no longer wanted or needed. Once in Montreal when 'He prepared to return to the Maxwells' home for a meeting, the friends asked if they could call a carriage for Him. 'Abdu'l-Bahá took the streetcar, saying, "Oh, it matters little. It saves expenses. There is a difference of one dollar in the fare." When He arrived at the Maxwells', He gave one pound to each of the servants.'[64] After spending two nights at the estate of Phoebe Hearst, He gathered the servants together and thanked them – each received ten dollars.

48

A certain lady witnessed a touching scene in Dublin, U.S.A. She was in the same inn where the Master was staying. 'Abdu'l-Bahá was out with His secretary. A poor, old man passed the inn and the Master asked the secretary to call him back. The man was not only ragged but filthy, but the Master took his hand and smiled at him. They talked together a moment, the Master taking in the whole figure – the man's trousers hardly served their purpose. The Master laughed gently and stepped into a shadow. The street was quite deserted. He fumbled with the clothes at His waist. When He stopped, His trousers slid down, but He drew His robe around His body and handed His trousers to the poor man with a 'May God go with you.'[65]

Magnanimity

'Abdu'l-Bahá's magnanimity was felt not only by His friends (of course), but also by His ill-wishers. He knew 'malice toward none'. He sweetened the lives of all with whom He came in contact, returning good for evil. Who better than He could thus advise His friends: '. . . never be defeated by the malice of the people, by their aggression and their hate, no matter how intense. If others hurl their darts against you, offer them milk and honey in return; if they poison your lives, sweeten their souls; if they injure you, teach them how to be comforted; if they inflict a wound upon you, be a balm to their sores; if they sting you, hold to their lips a refreshing cup.'[66]

'Should any come to blows with you, seek to be friends with him; should any stab you to the heart, be ye a healing salve unto his sores; should any taunt and mock at you, meet him with love. Should any heap his blame upon you, praise ye him; should he offer you a deadly poison, give him the choicest honey in exchange . . . should he be thorns, be ye his roses and sweet herbs.'[67]

49

One of the members of the 'ill-fated Commission of Inquiry, despatched from Constantinople to seal the fate of 'Abdu'l-Bahá', managed later to escape to Egypt, but was robbed by his servant on the way. The Bahá'ís in Cairo gave him financial help, which he had requested. Subsequently he asked help from 'Abdu'l-Bahá Himself. The Master 'immediately directed the believers to present him with a sum on His behalf, an instruction which they were unable to carry out owing to his sudden disappearance.'[68]

50

There was a time when the Covenant-Breakers 'gave away the garments and personal effects of Bahá'u'lláh to government functionaries, to serve as chattels of bribery and to provide as well the means of humiliating 'Abdu'l-Bahá. At their instigation the Deputy-Governor of Haifa would, whilst visiting 'Abdu'l-Bahá, ostentatiously wear Bahá'u'lláh's cloak and brazenly use His spectacles. Before long this man was dismissed from his post and fell on evil days. Then he went to 'Abdu'l-Bahá and begged

His forgiveness. He had acted, he said, in the manner he did, because he was prompted by 'Abdu'l-Bahá's own relatives. The Master showed him utmost kindness and generosity . . .'[69]

51

A similar story concerns an unkind governor of 'Akká, who attempted to destroy the livelihood of the honest and peace-loving Bahá'í shopkeepers by locking up their stores. However, when the plan was discovered, 'Abdu'l-Bahá asked those Bahá'ís not even to open their stores. Frustrated, the governor then received word that he was being deposed as governor and should be taken by the police to Damascus. In fear, he went to his home to prepare for this unexpected journey. The Master heard the news and went to him, offering His services. The ex-governor was worried about his family, wishing that they might also go to Damascus. 'Abdu'l-Bahá assured him that they would be sent to him. The Master provided a reliable escort, mules and all that was needed for a comfortable trip. The escort on arrival in Damascus would accept neither money nor gift – he wished only to obey the instructions of the Master. The governor could, however, write a letter to 'Abdu'l-Bahá and this he did immediately. It read, 'O 'Abdu'l-Bahá, I pray you pardon me. I did not understand. I did not know you. I have wrought you great evil. You have rewarded me with great good.'[70]

52

Another governor of 'Akká was dismissed from his duties and sent to Beirut to a new post. He had been very unkind and had not permitted the Bahá'ís to visit their Master, but with characteristic big-heartedness, 'Abdu'l-Bahá, hearing of his dismissal from his post in Beirut, sent a messenger with His good wishes and a gift of a 'very precious ring'. 'Abdu'l-Bahá, still a prisoner, offered to do what He could to be of assistance to him.[71]

53

When the Master was in the Chicago area, he visited Oak Woods Cemetery, to be at the grave site of Davis True. He was accompanied by Corinne True and others. As well as reciting the Prayer for the Dead, He also prayed for all the other people who were buried there.[72]

54

Julia Grundy once heard the Master tell a little-known story: 'The disciples of Jesus, passing along the road and seeing a dead dog, remarked how offensive and disgusting a spectacle it was. Then Christ turning to them said, "Yes, but see how white and beautiful are his teeth" – thus teaching that there is some good in everything.'[73] So, too, He taught that one should always look for the good and not for the bad. Life should be approached positively.

Thoughtfulness

55

On pilgrimage May Maxwell came to realize that every word and every act of the Master's had meaning and purpose. The pilgrim party was invited to meet 'Abdu'l-Bahá 'under the cedar trees on Mount Carmel where He had been in the habit of sitting with Bahá'u'lláh.' She recalled that 'on Sunday morning we awakened with the joy and hope of the meeting on Mount Carmel. The Master arrived quite early and after looking at me, touching my head and counting my pulse, still holding my hand He said to the believers present: "There will be no meeting on Mount Carmel to-day . . . we could not go and leave one of the beloved of God alone and sick. We could none of us be happy unless all the beloved were happy." We were astonished. That anything so important as this meeting in that blessed spot should be cancelled because one person was ill and could not go seemed incredible. It was so contrary to all ordinary habits of thought and action, so different from the life of the world where daily events and material circumstances are supreme in importance that it gave us a genuine shock of surprise, and in that shock the foundations of the old order began to totter and fall. The Master's words had opened wide the door of God's Kingdom and given us a vision of that infinite world whose only law is love. This was but one of many times that we saw 'Abdu'l-Bahá place above every other consideration the love and kindness, the sympathy and compassion due to every soul. Indeed, as we look back upon that blessed time spent in His presence we understand that the object of our pilgrimage was to learn for the first time on earth what love is, to witness its light in every face, to feel its burning heat in every heart and to become ourselves enkindled with this divine flame from the Sun of Truth, the Essence of whose being is love.'[74]

Consideration

56

An American family once wrote to the Master, asking if they might visit Him. 'Abdu'l-Bahá, who had travelled so far without comforts, replied, 'When you may travel in comfort, then you may come.' So, in 1919, after the first World War, it was arranged that the Randalls, along with others, should start for Haifa, in Palestine.[75]

57

Under a grove of trees near Lake Michigan, while in Chicago in 1912, 'Abdu'l-Bahá gave intimate and loving counsel to His friends: 'Some of you may have observed that I have not called attention to any of your individual shortcomings. I would suggest to you, that if you shall be similarly considerate in your treatment of each other, it will be greatly conducive to the harmony of your association with each other.'[76]

Compassion

58

On one occasion the Master reminded His friends as follows: 'We must execute the divine ordinances. The Blessed Beauty says, "If you have a word or a truth, which others are deprived of, present it with utmost compassion. If it is accepted, the aim is attained. If otherwise, you should not interfere. Leave him to himself, while advancing to God, the Mighty, the Self-subsisting." '[77]

59

One day, in London, while several people were talking to 'Abdu'l-Bahá, a man's voice was heard at the door. It was the son of a country clergyman, but now he looked more like an ordinary tramp and his only home was along the banks of the river Thames. He had walked thirty miles to see 'Abdu'l-Bahá. The man was taken to the dining-room, he was given food, and after he had rested for a while, he said, 'Last evening I had decided to put an end to my futile, hateful life, useless to God and man! In a little country town yesterday, whilst taking what I had intended should be my last walk, I saw *a Face* in the window of a newspaper shop. I stood looking at the face as if rooted to the spot. He seemed to speak to me, and call me to Him! . . . I read that He is here, in this house. I said to myself, "If there is on earth that personage, I shall take up again the burden of my life." . . . Tell me, is He here? Will He see me? Even me?' The lady replied, 'Of course He will see you . . .'

Just then 'Abdu'l-Bahá Himself opened the door,

extending His hands as though to a dear friend whom He was expecting. ' "Welcome! Most welcome! I am very much pleased that thou hast come. Be seated." Trembling the poor man sank into a chair by the Master. "Be happy! Be happy! . . . Do not be filled with grief . . . " encouraged the Master. "Though thou be poor, thou mayest be rich in the Kingdom of God." '

'Abdu'l-Bahá spoke these and other words of comfort, strength and healing. The man's cloud of misery seemed to melt away in the warmth of the Master's loving presence. Before the man left, he said that he was going to work in the fields, and that after he had saved a little money, he was going to buy some land to grow violets for the market.[78]

Concern

60

The Master's concern for others endured to the very end of His earthly life. During the afternoon of 27 November 1921, 'Abdu'l-Bahá sent His friends to the Shrine of the Báb to celebrate the Day of the Covenant. His family had tea with Him. He 'received with His unfailing courtesy and kindness that same afternoon, and despite growing weariness, the Muftí of Haifa, the Mayor and the Head of the Police . . .'[79] That evening 'He asked after the health of every member of the Household, of the pilgrims and of the friends in Haifa. "Very good, very good" He said when told that none were ill. This was His very last utterance concerning His friends.'[80]

Courtesy and Graciousness

61

One day the Master, with one of His daughters, approached a native woman, dirty and almost savage-looking. Hers had been a hard life as the daughter of a desert chief. Though she was not a Bahá'í, she quite naturally loved the Master, who was so genuinely kind. Lingering a moment, she bowed and greeted the Master. Kindly He made reply and, somehow knowing her need, 'pressed a coin into her hand' as He passed by. Obviously, she was filled with appreciation.

One of the Master's daughters told an observer that this woman had, in that brief encounter, said to the Master that 'she would pray for Him', and graciously He had thanked her.[81]

62

Howard Colby Ives observed, 'I have before spoken of His unfailing courtesy. It was really more than what that term usually connotes to the Western mind. The same Persian word is used for both reverence and courtesy. He "saw the Face of His Heavenly Father in every face" and reverenced the soul behind it. How could one be discourteous if such an attitude was held towards everyone!

'The husband of 'Abdu'l-Bahá's hostess in Dublin, who, while never becoming an avowed believer, had many opportunities of meeting and talking with the Master, when asked to sum up his impressions of Him, responded, after a little consideration: "I think He is the most perfect gentleman I have ever known." '[82]

Hospitality

63

In 'Abdu'l-Bahá's household, in addition to Himself, His wife, His sister, two married daughters with husbands and children, and His two youngest daughters, there were some orphan children and widows of martyrs. Mary Lucas observed that: 'These serve in some capacity in the household, and the sentiment of love and equality in every member of this home is a living example for the world. Everything is done in the spirit of love.'[83]

64

Corinne True recorded what she observed on an early pilgrimage: 'Arising early I went into the living room where the Master meets with His family every morning between six and seven o'clock. The widow of one of the martyrs sits on the floor in the Persian style and makes and serves the tea every morning. Her husband was one of three brothers who were imprisoned for this Cause. For days they had no news about them. One day they heard a great noise in the street and looking out they saw three heads placed on long poles and being carried through the streets, and when in front of their home they tossed these heads into their mother's room. She wiped them off with water and then threw them back, saying, "What I have given to God I will not take back." This woman who makes the tea had been married only one year to one of these brothers. Having lost all of her relatives through the persecution, and Persian women having no openings for self-support, the Master took her into His household. What a wonderful household this is –

over forty people living here in one home, some black, some white, Arabic, Persian, Burmanese, Italian, Russian and now English and American! Not a loud command is heard and not one word of dispute; not one word of fault-finding. Every one goes about as if on tip toes. When they enter your room, their slippers are left before the door and they come in with stocking feet and remain standing until you invite them to sit down.'[84]

65

Another early pilgrim was aware of the 'bitter antagonism' which ordinarily existed among the followers of different religious bodies. 'For example, a Jew and a Mohammedan would refuse to sit at meat together: a Hindu to draw water from the well of either. Yet, in the house of 'Abdu'l-Bahá we found Christians, Jews, Mohammedans, Zoroastrians, Hindus, blending together as children of the one GOD, living in perfect love and harmony.'[85]

Tenderness

66

Bahíyyih Randall* was only thirteen years old when she went to Haifa to see the Master. She recalled that 'there was a perfectly wonderful person who always sat on the right of 'Abdu'l-Bahá at dinner. His name was Ḥaydar-'Alí and he had been a follower of Bahá'u'lláh and was so meek and so beautiful. His hands would shake so that he could not eat. He was such an old, old man, and

* Bahíyyih Randall Ford Winckler. See anecdote 23.

'Abdu'l-Bahá would feed him with such tenderness. One day I saw him sitting out in the garden and I asked him what he had ever done. Of course, he could not speak English and I could not speak Persian, but we somehow seemed to understand. A man came along to interpret just then, and I told him what I had asked: 'What have you done to serve the Faith?'

'Ḥaydar-'Alí looked up with his eyes to heaven and said, "I have not done as much as an ant could do in the path of God." Then the interpreter told me that he had been dragged across the desert, tied in a bag on a camel, and that his whole life had been one series of martyrdoms – yet he had said, "I have not done as much as an ant could do in the path of God!" '[86]

Love

There is no need to belabour the fact that 'Abdu'l-Bahá's every act spoke of love – a love for every human being, each created by God. His abundant love, universal and divine, transcended limited, 'semi-selfish' loves – loves often born of race or religion, colour or country, family or friendship. Because His love of God and Bahá'u'lláh ran deep, His love for human beings followed naturally and sincerely. He knew what it meant when He said: 'When you love a member of your family or a compatriot, let it be with a ray of the Infinite Love! Let it be in God, and for God!'[87]

He advised pilgrim Anna Kunz and her husband in 1921, 'Just like a shepherd who is affectionate to all his sheep, without preference or distinction, you should be affectionate to all. You should not look at their shortcomings. Consider that they are all created by God who loves them all.'[88]

67

Once when 'Abdu'l-Bahá was asked, 'What is a Bahá'í?', He replied, 'To be a Bahá'í simply means to love all the world; to love humanity and try to serve it; to work for universal peace and universal brotherhood.'[89]

68

Gloria Faizi has beautifully explained the Master's wide love: 'When the heart of man is attracted to God through His Manifestation on earth, he has established a link of love with his Creator. And as the link grows stronger, he will feel an overflowing love for all that God has created. 'Abdu'l-Bahá once gave the example of a soiled and crushed letter that reaches the hand of a lover from his beloved. That letter, He said, is no less precious because of the condition in which it has arrived. It is cherished because it has come from a loved one. In the same way, we can learn to love a fellow man, no matter who he is, because he is God's creature.'[90]

69

One day, in London, 'Abdu'l-Bahá was out driving with Lady Blomfield and Mrs Thornburgh-Cropper, the first Bahá'í in England. Mrs Cropper asked Him, 'Master, are you not longing to be back at Haifa with your beloved family?' He smiled and replied: 'I wish you to understand that you are both as truly my dear daughters, as beloved by me, as are those of whom you speak.'[91]

70

Once 'Abdu'l-Bahá was asked, 'Why do all the guests who visit you come away with shining countenances?'

'He said with his beautiful smile: "I cannot tell you, but in all those upon whom I look, I see only my Father's Face." '92

71

The Master always responded to love with love. During a luncheon in London a gift arrived from Persia. A traveller, having passed through 'Ishqábád, in Russian Turkistán, was approached by a poor labourer, who, knowing he was going to see the Master, longed to send Him a gift – he had nothing but his own dinner. Lovingly, this was wrapped in a cotton handkerchief. Graciously, 'Abdu'l-Bahá now received the handkerchief, which He quickly untied. The black bread was dry, the apple shrivelled, but the Master did not touch His recently prepared luncheon. He ate instead of this humble food and shared it with His guests, saying, 'Eat with Me of this gift of humble love.'93

72

Into the lives of those He loved spilled 'Abdu'l-Bahá's love of flowers, which He often shared with others. On one occasion a 'little floor maid emerged from 'Abdu'l-Bahá's suite, her arms filled with roses – beautiful roses – a gift to Him from some of the Bahá'ís. Sensing that we were friends of the Master,' continued Ella Quant, 'all formality fell away and with a touching gesture she exclaimed, "See what He gave me! See what He gave *me*!" She probably knew nothing of 'Abdu'l-Bahá's Station as the Center of God's Covenant and the Interpreter of Bahá'u'lláh's teaching to a needy world; she perhaps did not know His name or title, but He had shown her His love.'[94]

73

To a minister who came to call on the Master in the Maxwell Home in Montreal, ' 'Abdu'l-Bahá presented an armful of gorgeous American Beauty roses, standing in a tall vase at His side, sending him away with amazement and awe at the regal manners and gentle courtesy of this Prisoner from the East.'[95]

74

Leroy Ioas,* a young boy in 1912, was blessed to meet the Master on His visit to Chicago. One day, on the way to the Plaza Hotel to hear 'Abdu'l-Bahá, he decided to buy Him some flowers. Though he had but little money, he managed to find a large bouquet of flowers which he himself especially liked – white carnations! But in approaching the hotel, he had a change of heart: he would not give 'Abdu'l-Bahá those flowers after all, he told his father. His dad was genuinely perplexed. Why, when the Master so loved flowers? Young Leroy gave his answer: 'I come to the Master offering Him my heart, and I do not want Him to think I want any favours. He knows what's in a person's heart, and that is all I have to offer.'

With that for an answer Leroy's father went upstairs and presented the flowers to 'Abdu'l-Bahá. How the

* Later appointed a Hand of the Cause by the Guardian in 1951.

Master enjoyed them! Their fragrance delighted Him and He buried His face in their midst, as He was inclined to do.

During the talk, Leroy sat at the feet of this great Teacher, completely fascinated. Those dynamic, ever-changing eyes! Those 'majestic movements'! That charm!

After the talk, the Master stood up and shook hands with each guest. To each He gave one white carnation. Finally only a few remained. Leroy, standing behind 'Abdu'l-Bahá, thought, 'Gee, I wish He would turn around and shake hands with me before they are all gone!' With that thought, the Master turned and saw him. 'Abdu'l-Bahá wore a lovely, red rose, which He then pulled from His coat and gave to the boy. Leroy knew the Master was aware that it was actually he who had brought those carnations.[96]

75

The Master loved children and took great delight in them. He felt 'they were nearer to the Kingdom of God' than were adults.[97]

It was observed how He listened so attentively one day to a young granddaughter of His – He took her troubles seriously. Though she was only about two years old, she chanted a Tablet in His presence. If a word failed her, He 'gently' chanted it. She won from Him a glorious smile for her effort, while He sat in the corner of the divan drinking tea.[98]

76

One July evening in 1919 a pilgrim held a sumptuous banquet at Bahjí. 'Abdu'l-Bahá Himself served about forty guests. Bedouins camping nearby also received a generous share. When their children came, the Master gave a coin to each. In the morning their fathers came to the Master, who was sitting in the garden by the Shrine of Bahá'u'lláh, writing Tablets, to express their appreciation and to seek His blessing.[99]

77

One day when the Master was out on a carriage ride near Thonon-les-Bains on Lake Geneva in France, the party stopped for simple refreshments at an old inn nestled between two mountains. Sitting on an open porch, 'Abdu'l-Bahá was soon spotted by children, who were selling bunches of violets and seemed to have eyes only for Him. They clustered around Him. Spontaneously He dug into His pocket and came out with some francs to satisfy His small salesfolk.[100]

78

The following delightful story about an incident during 'Abdu'l-Bahá's stay in New York illustrates the fact that He was not 'colour-blind', but rather He found racial differences a thing of beauty. When the Master was on His way to speak to several hundred men at the Bowery Mission He was accompanied by a group of Persian and American friends. Not unnaturally a group of boys was intrigued by the sight of this group of Orientals with their flowing robes and turbans and started to follow them. They soon became noisy and obstreperous. A lady in the Master's party was highly embarrassed at the rude behaviour of the boys. Dropping behind she stopped to talk with them and told them a little about who 'Abdu'l-Bahá was. Not entirely expecting them to take her up on the invitation, she nevertheless gave them her home address and said that if they liked to come the following Sunday she would arrange for them to see Him.

Thus, on Sunday, some twenty or thirty of them appeared on the doorstep, rather scruffy and noisy, but with signs that they had tidied up for the occasion nonetheless. Upstairs in 'Abdu'l-Bahá's room the Master was seen at the door greeting each boy with a handclasp or an arm around the shoulder, with warm smiles and boyish laughter. His happiest welcome seemed to be directed to the thirteen-year-old boy near the end of the line. He was quite dark-skinned and didn't seem too sure he would be welcome. The Master's face lighted up and in a loud voice that all could hear exclaimed with delight that 'here was a black rose'. The boy's face shone with happiness and love. Silence fell across the room as the boys looked at their companion with a new awareness.

The Master did not stop at that, however. On their arrival He had asked that a big five-pound box of delicious chocolates be fetched. With this He walked around the room, ladling out chocolates by the handful to each boy. Finally, with only a few left in the box, He picked out one of the darkest chocolates, walked across the room and held it to the cheek of the black boy. The Master was radiant as He lovingly put His arm around the boy's shoulders and looked with a humorously piercing glance around the group without making any further comment.[101]

89

79

Mr Robert Turner, the butler of philanthropist Mrs
Phoebe Hearst, distinguished himself by being the first
Western black man to become a Bahá'í. May Maxwell
recalled later that 'on the morning of our arrival [on
pilgrimage], after we had refreshed ourselves, the Master
summoned us all to Him in a long room overlooking the
Mediterranean. He sat in silence gazing out of the
window, then looking up He asked if all were present.
Seeing that one of the believers was absent, He said,
"Where is Robert?" . . . In a moment Robert's radiant
face appeared in the doorway and the Master rose to greet
him, bidding him be seated, and said, "Robert, your
Lord loves you. God gave you a black skin, but a heart
white as snow." '[102] 'Such was the tenacity of his faith
that even the subsequent estrangement of his beloved
mistress from the Cause she had spontaneously
embraced failed to becloud its radiance, or to lessen the
intensity of the emotions which the loving-kindness
showered by 'Abdu'l-Bahá upon him had excited in his
breast.'[103]

Service, Commitment, Involvement

Service to God, to Bahá'u'lláh, to family, to friends and
enemies, indeed to all mankind – this was the pattern of
'Abdu'l-Bahá's life. He wished only to be the Servant of
God and man. To serve – rather than being demeaning
and unfulfilling – was honour, joy and fulfilment. This
motivated His entire day from dawn to after midnight.
He used to say, 'Nothing is too much trouble when one
loves, and there is always time.'[104]

80

Howard Colby Ives recalled one meal at which ' 'Abdu'l-Bahá served me with His own hands most bountifully, urging me to eat, eat, be happy. He Himself did not eat but paced regally around the table, talking, smiling, serving.'[105] Later he wrote that 'He has been known to go into the kitchen and prepare a meal for His guests. He never failed in such small attentions as seeing that the room where His visitors were entertained contained every possible comfort, though He paid no attention to His own comfort.' His response when He was at one time asked to act as honorary chairman of a Bahá'í Assembly was simply, ' 'Abdu'l-Bahá is a servant.'[106]

81

One day when Lua Getsinger was in 'Akká to see the Master, 'He said to her, that He was too busy today to call upon a friend of His who was very ill and poor and He wished her to go in His place. Take him food and care for him as I have been doing, He concluded. He told her where this man was to be found and she went gladly, proud that 'Abdu'l-Bahá should trust her with this mission.

'She returned quickly. "Master," she exclaimed, "surely you cannot realize to what a terrible place you sent me. I almost fainted from the awful stench, the filthy rooms, the degrading condition of that man and his house. I fled lest I contract some terrible disease."

'Sadly and sternly 'Abdu'l-Bahá regarded her. "Dost thou desire to serve God," He said, "serve thy fellow man for in him dost thou see the image and likeness of God." He told her to go back to this man's house. If it is filthy she should clean it; if this brother of yours is dirty, bathe him; if he is hungry, feed him. Do not return until this is done. Many times had He done this for him and cannot she serve him once?'[107]

82

Before His wedding day, 'Abdu'l-Bahá made the necessary arrangements for the few guests. His mother and sister made a delicate bridal dress of white batiste. A white head-dress adorned Munírih Khánum's hair, worn, as usual, in two braids.

At nine in the evening she went with the Greatest Holy Leaf into the presence of Bahá'u'lláh, Who gave her His blessing. She then went to the bridal room and awaited the coming of 'Abdu'l-Bahá. The service was very simple. At about ten o'clock 'Abdu'l-Bahá came, accompanied by the guests, and Munírih Khánum chanted a Tablet revealed by Bahá'u'lláh. 'Later, the wife of 'Abbúd recalled the sweetness of that chanting still ringing in her ears.'[108]

There were no choir, decorations or cake – just cups of tea. Above all, a glory and a love there were more than sufficient to bless the happy event.

83

Elizabeth Gibson Cheyne, poetess, and her husband, Dr T. K. Cheyne, esteemed critic, lived in Oxford, England, when 'Abdu'l-Bahá visited them. Dr Cheyne's health and strength were waning. 'The beautiful loving care of the devoted wife for her gifted, invalid husband touched the heart of 'Abdu'l-Bahá. With tears in His kind eyes He spoke of them' to His companions on their way back to London, '"She is an angelic woman, an example to all in her unselfish love. Yes, she is a perfect woman. An angel."'[109]

84

One day in early May 1912, 'Abdu'l-Bahá travelled by train from Pittsburgh, Pennsylvania, to Washington, D.C. – a twelve-hour ride. 'His companions begged Him to take a special compartment or a berth on the train; but He refused saying, "I spend money only to help people and to serve the Cause of God; and I have never liked distinctions since my childhood."'[110]

Justice

'Abdu'l-Bahá's love in no way obscured His sense of justice. On the contrary: it heightened His awareness. Had not Bahá'u'lláh taught Him well that 'The best beloved of all things in My sight is Justice'?[111]

The Master Himself, speaking of justice, declared that: 'Its operation must be carried out in all classes, from the highest to the lowest. Justice must be sacred, and the rights of all the people must be considered. Desire for others only that which you desire for yourselves.'[112]

85

Economic justice, even in small matters, was important to the Master. Once in Egypt 'Abdu'l-Bahá obtained a carriage in order that He might offer a ride to an important Páshá, who was to be His luncheon guest. When they reached their destination, the driver asked an exorbitant fee. The Master was fully aware of this and refused to pay the full amount. The driver, big and rough, grabbed His sash and 'jerked Him back and forth', demanding his unfair price. 'Abdu'l-Bahá remained firm and the man eventually let go. The Master paid what He actually owed him and informed him that had he been honest, he would have received a handsome tip instead of only the fare. He then walked away.

Shoghi Effendi, His grandson, was present when this happened. He later admitted to being very embarrassed that this should have happened in front of the Páshá. 'Abdu'l-Bahá, on the other hand, was evidently 'not at all upset', but simply determined not to be cheated.[113]

Equality

In the twentieth century much is being said and written about the importance of human rights, but, already in 1875, 'Abdu'l-Bahá had written: '. . . have regard for the rights of others.'[114] His Father's Faith proclaimed the oneness of all mankind; the abolition of prejudices; the equality of men and women.

86

While 'Abdu'l-Bahá was living in a Paris hotel, among those who often came to see Him was a poor, black man. He was not a Bahá'í, but he loved the Master very much. One day when he came to visit, someone told him that the management did not like to have him – a poor black man – come, because it was not consistent with the standards of the hotel. The poor man went away. When 'Abdu'l-Bahá learned of this, He sent for the man

responsible. He told him that he must find His friend –
He was not happy that he should have been turned away.
'Abdu'l-Bahá said, 'I did not come to see expensive hotels
or furnishings, but to meet My friends. I did not come to
Paris to conform to the customs of Paris, but to establish
the standard of Bahá'u'lláh.'[115]

87

On a certain occasion in America 'Abdu'l-Bahá
'announced that He wished to give a Unity Feast for the
friends. The Committee arranging for the affair had
taken it to one of the city's most exclusive hotels, famed
for its color bar. The colored friends, troubled by the
prospect of insults and discriminatory treatment, decided
not to attend. When 'Abdu'l-Bahá learned of this, He
insisted that all the friends should attend. The banquet
was held with all the friends, white and colored, seated
side by side, in great happiness and without one
unpleasant incident.'[116]

88

In late May 1912, in New York, ' 'Abdu'l-Bahá was
evicted from His hotel because, as Maḥmúd noted, of
the "coming and going of diverse people" and the
"additional labors and troubles" for the staff and the
"incessant inquiries" directed to the hotel management.
"But," Maḥmúd continued, "when the people of the
hotel saw His great kindness and favor at the time of His
departure, they were ashamed of their conduct and
begged Him to stay longer, but He would not
accept."'[117]

89

The Master's every act was meaningful. On one auspicious occasion in Washington, D.C. He demonstrated what justice and love can do. The chargé d'affaires of the Persian Legation in the city and his wife had arranged a luncheon in His honour. Their guest list included members of the social and political life in the capital, as well as a number of Bahá'ís.

Louis Gregory, a cultivated gentleman and employee in the government – he later became the first black Hand of the Cause – had been invited to visit the Master. He was surprised at the time scheduled for a visit, as he knew of the luncheon plans, but naturally he arrived on time. Their conference seemed to go on and on – as if indeed the Master might be prolonging it deliberately.

Eventually the butler announced that luncheon was being served. 'Abdu'l-Bahá led the way, the invited guests following closely behind. Mr Gregory was perplexed: should he leave or wait for 'Abdu'l-Bahá to return? The guests were seated when suddenly the honoured Guest rose, looked around and then asked in English, 'Where is My friend, Mr Gregory?', adding 'My friend, Mr Gregory, must lunch with Me!' It just so happened that Louis Gregory had not been on the luncheon list, so naturally he had remained behind. Now the chargé d'affaires hastened after him. The Master rearranged the place setting at His right, the seat of honour, of course – ignoring utterly the delicate laws of protocol – and the luncheon started only after Mr Gregory had been seated. Then, in a most natural manner, as if nothing at all unusual had happened in the capital that day in 1912, with tact and humour, the Master 'electrified the already startled guests' by talking about the unity of mankind.[118]

90

Louis Gregory was blessed with going on pilgrimage. Towards its end ' 'Abdu'l-Bahá summoned Louis Gregory and Louisa Mathew, a white English pilgrim. He questioned them, and, to their surprise, expressed the wish that they should join their lives together. In deference to His wishes they were married, and he sent them forth as a symbol of the spiritual unity, cooperation, dignity in relationships and service He desired for the races of mankind. That marriage presented many challenges. It brought all the obstacles to understanding and amity, and often cruel pressures. But it endured because the two souls it joined were ever guided and protected by a love beyond themselves and the pressures of the world. Theirs was a demonstration of the love which is prompted by the knowledge of God and reflected in the soul. They saw in each other the Beauty of God; and, clinging to this, they were sustained throughout the trials, the accidental conditions of life and the changes and chances of human experience.'[119]

91

'Abdu'l-Bahá's sense of justice and equality also embraced the quality of relationship between men and women. He once smilingly turned to the ladies in a group of listeners in America and said that, 'in Europe and America, many men worked very hard so that their wives could have luxuries. He related, again with a smile, the story of a husband and wife who once visited Him. Some dust had settled on the wife's shoes, and she told her husband peremptorily to wipe it off, which he dutifully did. Did she do the same for her husband,

'Abdu'l-Bahá had queried. No, had been the reply, she cleaned his clothes. But that was not equality, 'Abdu'l-Bahá had remarked. "Now, ladies," 'Abdu'l-Bahá said, "you must sometimes stand up for the rights of men." It was all said with good humour, but the lesson was plain: moderation in all things.'[120]

Moderation

'Abdu'l-Bahá often emphasized the importance of moderation, both for oneself and in one's relationship with others.

92

One day 'Abdu'l-Bahá learned that a lady had cut her lovely hair in order to contribute to the building of the House of Worship in Wilmette. He wrote to her with loving appreciation: 'On the one hand, I was deeply touched, for thou hadst sheared off those fair tresses of thine with the shears of detachment from this world and of self-sacrifice in the path of the Kingdom of God. And on the other, I was greatly pleased, for that dearly-beloved daughter hath evinced so great a spirit of self-sacrifice as to offer up so precious a part of her body in the pathway of the Cause of God. Hadst thou sought my opinion, I would in no wise have consented that thou shouldst shear off even a single thread of thy comely and wavy locks; nay, I myself would have contributed in thy name for the Mashriqu'l-Adhkár. This deed of thine is, however, an eloquent testimony to thy noble spirit of self-sacrifice.'[121]

93

Mr George Latimer, writing of a visit to the Master, quoted Him as saying, 'You must be very moderate. Consider the taste of the public. This is the best policy. Moderation, moderation. You must speak and write in such a manner as not to offend anyone. The Lord addressed Moses and Aaron saying, "When you go to Pharaoh, speak in a moderate, sweet language."'[122]

94

When Anna and Jakob Kunz were on pilgrimage in 1921, the Master said to them, 'Everything must be done moderately. Excess is not desirable. Do not go to extremes. Even in thinking do not go to excess but be moderate.'[123]

95

During part of the Master's trip East in the United States 'Again He would not take pullman accommodations, even though requested by the friends, saying that they should not be dependent on bodily comforts: "We must be equal to the hardships of traveling like a soldier in the path of Truth and not be slaves to bodily ease and comfort."'

The next night the little five-member body of people accompanying 'Abdu'l-Bahá apparently did not suggest pullman accommodations. Were these people learning to travel like soldiers 'in the path of Truth'? 'In any event 'Abdu'l-Bahá told them to reserve six berths for that night because too much austerity was not good. They

suggested that perhaps only one might be secured for
Him, and He replied, "No, we must share equally." '[124]

Truthfulness

For 'Abdu'l-Bahá truthfulness was as natural as breath-
ing. He spoke not to gain popularity, nor to tell people
what they wanted to hear. His words served to educate
and help the hearer, if he chose to listen. A few examples
of this constant way of life must suffice.

96

At one time a high official in the federal government of
the United States questioned 'Abdu'l-Bahá about the best
way to serve his people and his government. The Master
had a ready answer: 'You can best serve your country
. . . if you strive, in your capacity as a citizen of the
world, to assist in the eventual application of the
principle of federalism underlying the government of
your own country to the relationships now existing
between the peoples and nations of the world.'[125]

97

When 'Abdu'l-Bahá met Admiral Peary, North Pole
explorer, while the Master was in America, He said, 'I
hope you will explore the invisibilities of the
Kingdom.'[126]

98

At Leland Stanford Junior University, near the end of a long address, the Master asserted: 'We live upon this earth for a few days and then rest beneath it forever. So it is our graveyard eternally. Shall man fight for the tomb which devours him, for his eternal sepulchre? What ignorance could be greater than this? To fight over his grave; to kill another for his grave! What heedlessness! What a delusion!'[127]

99

The words of 'Abdu'l-Bahá contained many surprises – both pleasant and not so pleasant. Among such written words were these: 'If once this life should offer a man a sweet cup, a hundred bitter ones will follow; such is the condition of this world.'[128]

'Bring them [the children] up to work and strive, and accustom them to hardship.'[129]

'The Báb hath said that the people of Bahá must develop the science of medicine to such a high degree that they will heal illnesses by means of foods.'[130]

'When the friends do not endeavour to spread the message, they fail to remember God befittingly . . .'[131]

The Master scattered abroad the seeds of truth – seeds that slowly germinate and gradually bear their profitable and happy harvest.

Knowledge and Wisdom

100

'Abdu'l-Bahá possessed both knowledge and wisdom, in word and deed. We marvel at His ready knowledge of the obscure fact, such as the one about the sepulchre of Christ which 'remained lost and unknown for three hundred years, until the maidservant of God, Helen, the mother of Constantine arrived and discovered the sacred spot.'[132]

101

No mere mortal in His day could claim to be His teacher. He learned well and thoroughly. When, late in His life, Bahá'u'lláh took up residence at Bahjí, the Master remained in 'Akká to attend to a multitude of details, which otherwise might have distracted Bahá'u'lláh from His writing. But frequently the Master carried news to Bahjí. He then reported on religious questions He had encountered. It was observed that Bahá'u'lláh asked for His answers and then approved them with 'very good'.

His wisdom was as astonishing as His knowledge. The Master's profound wisdom coupled with His all-encompassing, tender love were capable of producing a revolution in the inner life of those with whom He came in contact. This revolution was a 'change of heart'. Horace Holley became 'conscious of a new sympathy for individuals and a new series of ties by which all men are joined in one common destiny.' He discovered that ' 'Abdu'l-Bahá restores man to his state a little lower than the angels.'[133]

102

When 'Abdu'l-Bahá was in Stuttgart, Germany, in 1913, He related an incident from His early childhood: 'It is good to be a spreader of the Teachings of God in childhood. I was a teacher in this Cause at the age of this child (eight or nine years). This reminds me of a story. There was a man, highly educated, but not a Bahá'í. I, but a child, was to make of him a believer. The brother of this man brought him to me. I stayed with him, to teach him. He said, "I am not convinced, I am not satisfied." I answered, "If water were offered to a thirsty one, he would drink and be satisfied. He would take the glass. But you are not thirsty. Were you thirsty, then you too would be satisfied. A man with seeing eyes sees. I can speak of the sun to every seeing one, and say it is a sign of the day; but a blind person would not be convinced because he cannot see the sun. If I say to a man with good hearing, listen to the beautiful music, he would then listen and be made happy thereby. But if you play the most beautiful music in the presence of a deaf man, he would hear nothing. Now go and receive seeing eyes and hearing ears, then I will speak further with you on this subject." He went; but later he returned. Then he understood and became a good Bahá'í. This happened when I was very young.'[134]

103

Early in the days of 'Abdu'l-Bahá's imprisonment in the barracks in 'Akká, news of His wisdom spread from a butcher's shop. He and a few of Bahá'u'lláh's companions had left the barracks to procure food and other necessary items from the markets. In the butcher's shop where the Master waited to be served, a Muslim and a Christian were apparently expounding the merits of their respective faiths. The Christian was winning the discussion. Thereupon, 'Abdu'l-Bahá entered the conversation and with simplicity and eloquence proved the validity of Islám to the satisfaction of the Christian. The news of this incident 'spread and warmed the hearts of many people of 'Akká towards the Master; this was the beginning of His immense popularity among the inhabitants of that city.'[135] There even came a time when the governor of the city, Aḥmad Big Tawfíq, sent his own son to 'Abdu'l-Bahá for instruction and enlightenment.

104

In 1914 the Master wrote to the friends in Denver concerning how to convey the message of Bahá'u'lláh: 'The three conditions of teaching the Cause of God are the science of sociability, purity of deeds and sweetness of speech. I hope each one of you may become confirmed with these three attributes.'[136]

Earlier in New York City, He had spoken to His friends about their going to Green Acre, the Bahá'í summer school in Maine: 'You must give the message through action and deed, not alone by word. Word must be conjoined with deed. You must love your friend better than yourself; yes, be willing to sacrifice yourself. The cause of Bahá'u'lláh has not yet appeared in this country. I desire that you be ready to sacrifice everything for each other, even life itself; then I will know that the cause of Bahá'u'lláh has been established. I will pray for you that you may become the cause of upraising the lights of God. May everyone point to you and ask "Why are these people so happy?" I want you to be happy in

'Abdu'l-Bahá with children in Washington D.C., November, 1912

'Abdu'l-Bahá speaking in the Plymouth Congregation Church, Chicago, 5 May 1912

Green Acre, to laugh, smile and rejoice in order that others may be made happy by you.'[137]

On the same subject He wrote: 'Caution and prudence, however, must be observed even as recorded in the Book. The veil must in no wise be suddenly rent asunder.'[138]

The teacher should also be concerned about the listener's physical needs. This practical approach was apparent in 'Abdu'l-Bahá's words: 'Never talk about God to a man with an empty stomach. Feed him first.'[139]

105

At one time the Master was asked, 'What shall I say to those who state that they are satisfied with Christianity and do not need this present Manifestation?' His reply was clear: 'Let them alone. What would they do if a former king had reigned and a new king was now seated upon the throne? They must acknowledge the new king, or they are not true subjects of the Kingdom. Last year there was a springtime. Can a man say "I do not need a new springtime this year – the old springtime is enough for me"? No! The new spring must come to fill the earth with beauty and brightness.'[140]

106

The Master's positive approach to life and to people encouraged His friends, good as they may have been, to become even better. They were to 'see no evil' in others, nor were they to see it in themselves, except in so far that it encouraged them to grow spiritually. The Master said, 'Do not look at thy weakness; nay look at the power of thy Lord, which hath surrounded all regions.'[141] This advice is found repeatedly: 'Do not look at your weakness, nay, rely upon the confirmation of the Holy Spirit. Verily, It maketh the weak strong, the lowly mighty, the child grown, the infant mature and the small great.'[142]

And again – 'Trust in the favor of God. Look not at your own capacities, for the divine bestowal can transform a drop into an ocean; it can make a tiny seed a lofty tree.'[143]

Super-psychiatrist that He was, He taught that, 'We should not be occupied with our failings and weakness, but concern ourselves about the Will of God so that It may flow through us, thereby healing these human infirmities.'[144]

107

Corinne True made one of her nine pilgrimages to the Bahá'í Holy Places in Palestine 'during the time of the Second Commission of Investigation by the Turks, when 'Abdu'l-Bahá had again been confined as a prisoner to 'Akká by order of the Sultán of Turkey. On this visit Mrs True took a petition to the Master asking permission for the American Bahá'ís to begin planning for the erection of a "House of Worship". This petition was in the form of a parchment containing the signatures of over a thousand American believers. She tells the story of putting the parchment behind her on the divan and first presenting the little gifts sent by the loving friends. But the Master strode across the room, reached behind her and grasped the parchment, holding it high in the air. "This," He exclaimed, "this is what gives me great joy." "Go back," He told her, "go back and work for the Temple; it is a great work." How she longed to do this work, but it seemed such a great task. 'Abdu'l-Bahá, looking at her with deep intensity said, "Devote yourself to this project – make a beginning, and all will come right." He then proceeded to give basic instructions about its design. It was to have nine sides, nine gardens, nine fountains, nine doors, nine walks, etc. And so a vision of the first Bahá'í Temple in the Western Hemisphere was born.'[145]

108

'Abdu'l-Bahá was in California in 1912 – a presidential election year. One October morning this election was mentioned during a conversation. The Master commented: 'The president must be a man who is not hankering for the presidency. He should be a person free from all thoughts of name and fame; he must think himself unworthy of the rank; and should say that he thinks himself unfit for the place and unable to bear this burdensome duty . . . If the public good is the object, the president must be a person sensitive to the public weal and not a selfish and self-seeking one.'[146]

109

For many years during the Master's late life there occurred a constant 'flow of pilgrims' who 'transmitted the verbal messages and special instructions of a vigilant Master'.[147] World War I brought a rude halt to these heavenly journeys.

'A remarkable instance of the foresight of 'Abdu'l-Bahá was supplied during the months immediately preceding the war. During peace times there was usually a large number of pilgrims at Haifa, from Persia and other regions of the globe. About six months before the outbreak of war one of the old Bahá'ís living at Haifa presented a request from several believers of Persia for permission to visit the Master. 'Abdu'l-Bahá did not grant the permission, and from that time onwards gradually dismissed the pilgrims who were at Haifa, so that by the end of July, 1914, none remained. When, in the first days of August, the sudden outbreak of the Great War startled the world, the wisdom of His precaution became apparent.'[148]

110

After the war, pilgrimages were resumed. Among the last of those fortunate pilgrims to visit 'Abdu'l-Bahá were the members of the Edwin Mattoon family. In their great longing to reach His side, they had asked if they might come from the United States 'if only for a day'. Permission was granted. With their two little daughters, Florence (Zmeskal) and Annamarie (Baker), the latter only three months old, they joyously set sail. They were asked to take a part of an automobile so that the Master's – sent by American friends – might be repaired. Somehow they managed that, too. Annie Mattoon remembered later that 'Abdu'l-Bahá said to them, 'You must never forget Christ.'[149] With this encouragement, they included visits to the Holy Places of Christianity. (Today, also, Bahá'ís frequently make the 'wider pilgrimage'.)

Chapter III

HIS RADIANT HEART

When a man turns his face to God he finds sunshine everywhere.[1]

The All-loving God created man to radiate the Divine light and to illumine the world by his words, action and life.[2]

Unless one accepts dire vicissitudes, not with dull resignation, but with radiant acquiescence, one cannot attain . . . freedom.[3]

'Abdu'l-Bahá

'Abdu'l-Bahá learned well the meaning of Bahá'u'lláh's words: 'Beware, lest thou allow anything whatsoever to grieve thee.'[4] Acquainted with sorrow, He was known to shed tears when He spoke of the hardships endured by Bahá'u'lláh, His family and His followers who went into exile with Him. Sometimes He appeared sad because not more people were responsive to His call to Bahá'u'lláh, but He truly lived what He spoke when He said, referring to the spiritual Kingdom, 'A man living with his thoughts in this Kingdom knows perpetual joy. The ills all flesh is heir to do not pass him by, but they only touch the surface of his life, the depths are calm and serene.'[5]

Happiness

I

Stanwood Cobb, the renowned educator, wrote, 'This philosophy of joy was the keynote of all of 'Abdu'l-Bahá's teaching. "Are you happy?" was His frequent greeting to His visitors. "Be happy!"

'Those who were unhappy (and who of us are not at times!) would weep at this. And 'Abdu'l-Bahá would smile as if to say, "Yes, weep on. Beyond the tears is sunshine."

'And sometimes He would wipe away with His own hands the tears from their wet cheeks, and they would leave His presence transfigured.'[6]

In California it was observed that 'despite the Master's fatigue at times, and His physical ailments, He welcomed everyone with a beaming smile, and in His pleasing and vibrant voice would ask, "Are you happy?" '[7]

2

A woman visited the Master in Haifa, in May 1910. She later wrote about this visit, saying: 'As He talked with me, I felt my heart soften under the influence of his goodness and kindness, and the tears came to my eyes. He asked me about myself, if I were well, and if I were happy. I replied to the latter question, "I have had many sorrows!" ' He replied, ' "Forget them! When your heart is filled with the love of God, there will not be room for sorrow, there will only be love and happiness." '

She continued, 'I cannot tell you the sweet sympathy of his voice as he said these beautiful and comforting words. Then he had the attendant bring in tea, a cup for him and a cup for me. We drank together, wishing each other health and happiness, and then he told me that he hoped he should take tea with me in the Kingdom of Heaven. (Was that not a pretty thought?) When I praised the tea, he said it was real Persian tea, and presented me with a package to take away with me.'[8]

3

To read the words of 'Abdu'l-Bahá on this subject, to hear their spiritual meaning and to bathe in their warmth, is to find deep inner joy and inspiration. A very few examples follow:

'Joy gives us wings! In times of joy our strength is more vital, our intellect keener, and our understanding less clouded. We seem better able to cope with the world and to find our sphere of usefulness. But when sadness visits us we become weak, our strength leaves us, our comprehension is dim and our intelligence veiled. The actualities of life seem to elude our grasp, the eyes of our spirits fail to discover the sacred mysteries, and we become even as dead beings.'[9]

'Never be depressed.'[10]

'Never is it the wish of 'Abdu'l-Bahá to see any being hurt, nor will He make anyone to grieve; for man can receive no greater gift than this, that he rejoice another's heart.'[11]

'Remember the saying: "Of all pilgrimages the greatest is to relieve the sorrow-laden heart." '[12]

'. . . know thou that delivering the Message can be accomplished only through goodly deeds and spiritual attributes, an utterance that is crystal clear and the happiness reflected from the face of that one who is expounding the Teachings.'[13]

'Strive then to the best of thine ability to let these

children know that a Bahá'í is one who embodieth all the perfections, that he must shine out like a lighted taper – not be darkness upon darkness and yet bear the name "Bahá'í".'[14]

'In a time to come, morals will degenerate to an extreme degree. It is essential that children be reared in the Bahá'í way, that they may find happiness both in this world and the next. If not, they shall be beset by sorrows and troubles, for human happiness is founded upon spiritual behaviour.'[15]

'As to spiritual happiness, this is the true basis of the life of man, for life is created for happiness, not for sorrow; for pleasure, not for grief. Happiness is life; sorrow is death. Spiritual happiness is life eternal. This is a light which is not followed by darkness. . . . This great blessing and precious gift is obtained by man only through the guidance of God . . .' 'This happiness is but the love of God.'[16]

'Nothing makes a man so happy as love.'[17]

4

To Mrs Smith, a new Bahá'í, who belonged to a distinguished Philadelphia family and who was suffering with a headache, the Master said, 'You must be happy always. You must be counted among the people of joy and happiness and must be adorned with divine morals. In a large measure happiness keeps our health while depression of spirit begets diseases. The substance of eternal happiness is spirituality and divine morality, which has no sorrow to follow it.'[18]

5

In New York 'Abdu'l-Bahá said, 'May everyone point to you and ask "Why are these people so happy?" I want you to be happy . . . to laugh, smile and rejoice in order that others may be made happy by you.'[19]

6

In Chicago the Master revealed 'one of His most buoyant Tablets', requested by a newspaper reporter:

> Be happy! Be happy! The Sun of Truth has shone!
> Be happy! Be happy! The Light of the Spirit has surrounded the world!
> Be happy! Be happy! The doors of the Kingdom are opened!
> Be happy! Be happy! The song of the Supreme Concourse is raised!
> Be happy! Be happy! The breaths of the Holy Spirit are life-giving and the world of man is being quickened.[20]

Those words remind us of another passage of His:

> Glad Tidings!
> For everlasting life is here.
> O ye that sleep, awake!
> O ye heedless ones, learn wisdom!
> O blind, receive your sight!
> O deaf, hear!
> O dumb, speak!
> O dead, arise!
> Be happy!
> Be happy!
> Be full of joy.[21]

7

In His great eagerness to make others happy – free of anxiety, frustration and grief – 'Abdu'l-Bahá left many prayers for our use. The following prayer is one of the most dearly loved:

'O God, Refresh and gladden my spirit. Purify my heart. Illumine my mind. I lay all my affairs in Thy hand. Thou art my Guide and my Refuge. I will no longer be sorrowful and grieved; I will be a happy and joyful being. O God! I will no longer be full of anxiety, nor will I let trouble harass me. I will not dwell on the unpleasant things of life. O God! Thou art kinder to me than I am to myself. I dedicate myself to Thee, O Lord.'[22]

8

The happiness the Master knew through Bahá'u'lláh He wished for others. One of the very first pilgrims to 'Akká from the Occident recalled her party's last interview with 'Abdu'l-Bahá: 'In the might and majesty of His presence, our fear was turned to perfect faith, our weakness into strength, our sorrow into hope, and ourselves forgotten in our love for Him. As we all sat before Him, waiting to hear His words, some of the believers wept bitterly. He bade them dry their tears, but they could not for a moment. So again He asked them for His sake not to weep, nor would He talk to us and teach us until all tears were banished. . . .'[23]

9

Two pilgrims had just arrived in 'Akká in January 1908, after a long journey in the midst of winter. They described their first meeting with the Master, only minutes after they had entered His home.

'He came at once, the joyous ring of His voice reaching us even before we saw Him, calling, "Welcome! Welcome! I am glad you are here!" and adding to His warm, strong hand-clasp, the greater welcome of His wonderful eyes and heavenly smile. He made us sit down with Him and immediately asked about the American believers. . . . When we mentioned those who had sent Him special greeting, His beautiful face beamed with happiness.'[24]

10

One day a despondent little Jewish girl, all in black, was brought into the Master's presence. With tears flowing, she told Him her tale of woes: her brother had been unjustly imprisoned three years before – he had four more years to serve; her parents were constantly depressed; her brother-in-law, who was their support, had just died. She claimed the more she trusted in God the worse matters became. She complained, '. . . my mother reads the Psalms all the time; she doesn't deserve that God should desert her so. I read the Psalms myself, – the ninety-first Psalm and the twenty-third Psalm every night before I go to bed. I pray too.'

Comforting and advising her, 'Abdu'l-Bahá replied, 'To pray is not to read Psalms. To pray is to trust in God, and to be submissive in all things to Him. Be submissive, then things will change for you. Put your family in God's hands. Love God's will. Strong ships are not conquered by the sea, – they ride the waves. Now be a strong ship, not a battered one.'[25]

II

A 'Mrs C' was an early believer who went to 'Akká. She belonged to a wealthy and fashionable group of people in New York. Her life had been conventional and rather unsatisfying. She had been a sincere Christian, but somehow had not gained much comfort from her religion. She had become somewhat melancholy. While travelling abroad, she had learned about 'Abdu'l-Bahá. She eagerly grasped His message and headed to the prison-city. Having arrived, she was fascinated by everything, most especially by the Master. She noticed that 'Abdu'l-Bahá always greeted her with 'Be happy!' The other members of the party were not addressed in the same way by Him. This troubled her. Finally she asked someone to ask the Master why He addressed her in this way. With 'His peculiarly illuminating smile', He replied, 'I tell you to be happy because we can not know the spiritual life unless we are happy!'

'Then Mrs C's dismay was complete, and her diffidence vanished with the fulness of her despair.

' "But tell me, what is the spiritual life?" she cried, "I have heard ever since I was born about the spiritual life, and no one could ever explain to me what it is!"

' 'Abdu'l-Bahá looked at His questioner again with that wonderful smile of His, and said gently: "Characterize thyself with the characteristics of God, and thou shalt know the spiritual life!" ' – few words, but they were sufficient. Mrs C began to wonder what 'Abdu'l-Bahá meant. The characteristics of God? They must be such attributes as love and beauty, justice and generosity.

'All day long her mind was flooded with the divine puzzle, and all day long she was happy. She did not give a thought to her duties, and yet when she arrived at the moment of her evening's reckoning, she could not remember that she had left them undone.

'At last she began to understand. If she was absorbed in Heavenly ideals, they would translate themselves into deeds necessarily, and her days and nights would be full of light. From that moment she never quite forgot the divine admonition that had been granted her: "Characterize thyself with the characteristics of God!"

'And she learned to know the spiritual life.'[26]

Spirituality

George Townshend, one-time Canon of St Patrick's Cathedral, in Dublin, Ireland and Archdeacon of Clonfort Cathedral, who became an ardent Bahá'í, wrote, 'Christ taught that the supreme human achievement is not any particular deed nor even any particular condition of mind: but a relation to God. To be completely filled – heart – mind – soul – with love for God, such is the great ideal, the Great Commandment. In 'Abbás Effendi's character the dominant element was spirituality. Whatever was good in His life He attributed not to any separate source of virtue in Himself but to the power and beneficence of God. His single aim was servitude to God. He rejoiced in being denuded of all earthly possessions and in being rich only in His love for God. He surrendered His freedom that He might become the bondservant of God; and was able at the close of His days to declare that He had spent all His strength upon the Cause of God. To Him God was the center of all existence here on earth as heretofore and hereafter. All things were in their degree mirrors of the bounty of God and outpourings of His power.'[27]

'Abdu'l-Bahá wrote, 'Souls are like unto mirrors, and the bounty of God is like unto the sun. When the mirrors pass beyond all coloring and attain purity and polish, and are confronted with the sun, they will reflect in full perfection its light and glory. In this condition one should not consider the mirror, but the power of the light of the sun, which hath penetrated the mirror, making it a reflector of the heavenly glory.'[28]

He also wrote, '. . . with the love of God every bitterness is changed into sweetness and every gift becometh precious.'[29]

Today humanity is increasingly concerned – and rightly so – with 'the quality of life'. 'Abdu'l-Bahá was absorbed with both its spiritual and its physical dimensions: He knew that as the quality of man's spiritual life improves, his physical life would improve also – the outer world reflects the inner man. He was fully aware that we are indeed on a 'spiritual journey from self to God'. He wanted all people to be aware of this vital fact also – then they could truly arise to their real potential, both in this world and in the next.

12

In 1911 in a little Boston suburb called Medford, a woman from London came to speak about the martyrs in the early days of the Bahá'í Faith. William Randall was one of the guests invited to the home of Marian Williams Conant. Mr Randall had never as much as heard of the Bahá'í Faith, yet he went with moderate interest. When the evening was over and he was shaking hands with the speaker, who had shown pictures of early martyrs, she looked at him and said, 'Mr Randall, you are the only person in this room who has caught the spirit of this evening. I am going to send someone to you to tell you of the Bahá'í Faith.'

Mr Randall was startled but thanked her and departed. A few weeks passed. One morning he looked up from his desk and saw Harlan Ober standing before him. He was immediately impressed with Harlan's eyes and with his sincerity. Having seated himself, Harlan began to tell him about the Bahá'í Faith.

Mr Randall had long had a lively interest in religion. Born a Catholic, he had become an Episcopalian, but he had gone into Theosophy, Christian Science and New Thought movements; he had studied ancient religions. He felt he knew all there was to know about religion. He had no real interest in studying a new faith now, but Mr Ober was persistent. As the months passed, Harlan Ober repeatedly dropped in on William Randall, urging him to study, telling him more about this new Faith.

When 'Abdu'l-Bahá came to Boston in 1912, Harlan said to his reluctant student, 'You must go and see Him . . .' Mr Randall was disinclined, but finally consented to hear the Master lecture in Boston. Listening to Him, he thought that this Man was certainly a very great Man, truly a Saint.

At the close of the lecture, as Mr Randall was leaving the hall, he heard one of 'Abdu'l-Bahá's secretaries ask, 'Is there anyone here who would be gracious enough to buy 'Abdu'l-Bahá some grape juice? He is very fond of it and would like some after His lecture.' Instinctively, Mr Randall replied, 'I would be very glad to get it.' At the corner drug store he bought six bottles of grape juice and took them to the hotel where the Master was staying. He could give them to someone who could take them to 'Abdu'l-Bahá, as he did not want to become involved. When he got off the elevator, he was drawn swiftly into conversation with friends who were standing near. Hardly realizing what he was doing, he handed his bottles to one of the Master's secretaries.

The next thing he knew the secretary returned with a glass of grape juice on a tray and said to Mr Randall, 'Since you have been so kind to bring this to 'Abdu'l-Bahá, won't you take it in yourself, Mr Randall?' Not liking the idea – yet not wishing to be ungracious – he consented, but planned to put it on the nearest table and make a speedy exit. He put aside the little curtain before the Master's door, saw just the right table and deposited his tray. Just as he was backing out, pleased that he had not disturbed 'Abdu'l-Bahá, who was all alone at the far side of the room, seemingly asleep, the Master opened His eyes and looking at him, said, 'Be seated'. Feeling that he could not well refuse, Mr Randall seated himself on a couch in the centre of the room. 'Abdu'l-Bahá settled again into His chair and closed His eyes. William Randall sat still for a few moments and then began to get angry, thinking the Master did not know in whose presence He was sitting. He became more and more angry. He wondered, 'What does it mean that I have to sit in the presence of this old Man while He falls asleep?'

He thought about getting up and leaving the room, but decided against this approach to his predicament. 'Abdu'l-Bahá had told him to sit there and he must not be rude. Then his legs began to go to sleep and grow numb. His whole body began to get numb. Even his collar, starched and stiff – he prided himself that it was never wilted in public – drooped down. At the peak of his rage, a voice inside him said, 'You have studied all the great religions of the world and what good have they done you, for you cannot sit in the presence of an old man for twenty minutes with peace and composure?'

As the challenge of this thought struck Mr Randall, 'Abdu'l-Bahá opened His eyes and said, 'The intellect is good but until it has become the servant of the heart, it is of little avail.' Then the Master smiled at Mr Randall and dismissed him. He had not been asleep. Mr Randall never forgot the Master's words – they were a turning point in his life.[30]

13

'The Japanese Ambassador to a European capital (Viscount Arawaka – Madrid) was staying at the Hôtel d'Jéna (in Paris). This gentleman and his wife had been told of 'Abdu'l-Bahá's presence in Paris, and the latter was anxious to have the privilege of meeting Him.

' "I am very sad," said Her Excellency. "I must not go out this evening as my cold is severe, and I leave early in the morning for Spain. If only there were a possibility of seeing Him."

'This was told to the Master, Who had just returned after a long, tiring day.

' "Tell the lady and her husband that, as she is unable to come to me, I will call upon her."

'Accordingly, though the hour was late, through the cold and the rain He came, with His smiling courtesy, bringing joy to us all, as we awaited Him in the Tapestry Room of the Hôtel d'Jéna.

' 'Abdu'l-Bahá talked with the Ambassador and his wife of conditions in Japan, of the great international importance of that country, of the vast service to mankind, of the work for the abolition of war, of the need for improving conditions of life for the worker, of the necessity of educating girls and boys equally. "The religious ideal is the soul of all plans for the good of mankind. Religion must never be used as a tool by party politicians. God's politics are mighty, man's politics are feeble."

'Speaking of religion and science, the two great wings with which the bird of human kind is able to soar, He said, "Scientific discoveries have increased material civilization. There is in existence a stupendous force, as yet, happily, undiscovered by man. Let us supplicate God, the Beloved, that this force be not discovered by science until spiritual civilization shall dominate the human mind. In the hands of men of lower material nature, this power would be able to destroy the whole earth." '[31]

His words proved prophetic, but it would be decades before they could be better understood.

14

Stanwood Cobb recorded that 'the most important interview' he had with the Master was while in Paris in 1913. He wrote, 'I was one of the staff of Porter Sargent's Travel School for Boys. On my first visit He inquired about the school and asked me what I taught. I told Him that I taught English, Latin, Algebra and Geometry. He gazed intently at me with His luminous eyes and said, "Do you teach the spiritual things?"

'This question embarrassed me. I did not know how to explain to 'Abdu'l-Bahá that the necessity of preparing the boys for college-entrance exams dominated the nature of the curriculum. So I simply answered: "No, there is not time for that."

' 'Abdu'l-Bahá made no comment on this answer. But He did not need to. Out of my own mouth I had condemned myself and modern education. *No time for spiritual things!* That, of course, is just what is wrong with our modern materialistic "civilization". It has no time to give for spiritual things.

'But 'Abdu'l-Bahá's question and His silent response

indicated that from His viewpoint spiritual things should come first.'[32]

15

The Master loved children. It was observed that 'many of His talks were given as He sat with His arm encircling one of them.' To parents He would speak in the following vein: 'Give this child a good education; make every effort that it may have the best you can afford, so that it may be enabled to enjoy the advantage of this glorious age. Do all you can to encourage spirituality in them.'[33]

16

One June day in New York 'Abdu'l-Bahá was tired and slept long enough to keep His audience waiting. He then told His friends, 'While I was sleeping I was conversing with you as though speaking at the top of My voice. Then through the effect of My Own voice I awoke. As I awoke, one word was upon My lips, – the word "Imtiyaz" (Distinction). So I will speak to you upon that subject this morning.'

Gifted, impromptu speaker that He was, He then proceeded to give a now dearly-loved and well-known speech. He pointed out that He was not desirous that the friends achieve ordinary worldly distinctions. At the very end came words fit for man to follow for centuries to come: 'For you I desire spiritual distinction; that is, you must become eminent and distinguished in morals. In the love of God you must become distinguished from all else. You must become distinguished for loving humanity; for unity and accord; for love and justice. In brief, you must become distinguished in all the virtues of the human world; for faithfulness and sincerity; for justice and fidelity; for firmness and steadfastness; for philanthropic deeds and service to the human world; for love toward every human being; for unity and accord with all people; for removing prejudices and promoting international peace. Finally, you must become distinguished for heavenly illumination and acquiring the bestowals of God. I desire this distinction for you.'[34]

17

One day in London the Master gave His listeners an unusual, imaginative, yet realistic dialogue between the Prophets and men: 'Always, man has confronted the Prophets with this: "We were enjoying ourselves, and living according to our own opinions and desires. We ate; we slept; we sang; we danced. We had no fear of God, no hope of Heaven; we liked what we were doing, we had our own way. And then you came. You took away our pleasures. You told us now of the wrath of God, again of the fear of punishment and the hope of reward. You upset our good way of life."

'The Prophets of God have always replied: "You were content to stay in the animal world, We wanted to make you human beings. You were dark, We wanted you illumined; you were dead, We wanted you alive. You were earthly, We wanted you heavenly."'[35]

18

One day, during the Master's visit to New York City, He paid a visit to Central Park. After spending several hours in the Museum of Natural History, He came out to rest under the trees. A solicitous little old watchman inquired, ' "Would you like to go back after you have rested? There are fossils and birds." ' 'Abdu'l-Bahá smiled and replied, ' "No, I am tired of going about looking at the things of this world. I want to go above and travel and see the spiritual worlds. What do you think about that?" ' The watchman scratched his head – he was puzzled. Then the Master queried, ' "Which would you rather possess, the material or the spiritual world?" ' ' "Well, I guess the material." ' ' "But," continued 'Abdu'l-Bahá, "you do not lose it when you attain the spiritual. When you go upstairs in a house you do not leave the house. The lower floor is under you." ' Suddenly the old man seemed to see the light.[36]

19

One day 'Abdu'l-Bahá sent for Julia Grundy, an early Bahá'í pilgrim to the Holy Land. His words were brimming with love and inspiration: 'I want you to carry away from 'Akká the joy and peace of the spiritual life.'[37]

'The true pleasure and happiness depend upon the spiritual perception and enjoyment. The powers of mind are the bounties of God given to man to lead him toward spiritual happiness. The highest grace in man is to love God. Love of God, Knowledge of God is the greatest, the only real happiness, because it is Nearness to God. This is the Kingdom of God. To love God is to know him. To know Him is to enter His Kingdom and be near Him. This is what I desire for you – that you may walk in this path.'[38]

20

Early in 1909 Charles and Mariam Haney, the parents of Hand of the Cause of God Paul Haney, went to 'Akká to see 'Abdu'l-Bahá. In 'A Heavenly Feast' they recorded some of the utterances they heard from the Master during those nine days. One day 'Abdu'l-Bahá asked about the health of Mr Haney. He told the Master quite frankly, 'My body is always well, but I am receiving so much Spiritual Food while here that I fear I shall have Spiritual indigestion.' But his Host assured him: 'No, you are going to digest it, for He who gives you the Spiritual Food is going to give you digestive power.'[39]

During those days 'Abdu'l-Bahá bade them 'remember that the essential health is Spiritual Health, for by means of Spiritual Health eternal life is obtained; whereas, through physical health only temporary results are obtained.'[40]

21

The Master sent a Tablet to a lady who longed 'for the Heavenly Kingdom'. In part, He wrote, 'Recite the Greatest Name at every morn, and turn thou unto the Kingdom of Abhá, until thou mayest apprehend my mysteries.'[41]

22

Lua Getsinger – spiritual mother of both Mrs Hearst and May Bolles (Maxwell) – was a member of a pilgrim group, late in 1898. For the following eighteen years she returned time and again to 'Akká and Haifa. 'Abdu'l-Bahá entrusted her with vital teaching missions, and constantly instructed her in the path of divine love.

During one of her visits to the Middle East, the Master told her, 'Thou must be firm and unshakable in thy purpose, and never, never let any outward circumstances worry thee. I am sending thee to India to accomplish certain definite results. Thou must enter that country with a never-failing spirituality, a radiant faith, an eternal enthusiasm, an inextinguishable fire, a solid conviction, in order that thou mayest achieve those services for which I am sending thee. Let not thy heart be troubled. If thou goest away with this unchanging condition of invariability of inner state, thou shalt see the doors of confirmation open before thy face, thy life will be a crown of heavenly roses, and thou shalt find thyself in the highest station of triumph.

'Strive day and night to attain to this exalted state. Look at me! Thou dost not know a thousandth part of the difficulties and seemingly unsurmountable passes that rise daily before my eyes. I do not heed them: I am walking in my chosen highway.'[42]

Lua grew impatient to grow spiritually. Impetuous by nature, she wanted instant perfection the better to serve 'Abdu'l-Bahá, but the Master taught her that she could not stand that – perfection is a slowly evolving process.

Her passion for her Faith and her love for the Master knew no bounds. The physical world became less important to her as she grew in spirituality. Even her style of dress changed before her premature death in 1916. She had abandoned her old finery. Instead she always wore a conservative blue outfit. During her last years she lived only in and for the world of the spirit.

Radiant Acquiescence

The Master's radiance will inspire men and women for centuries yet unborn. He was joyful when most people in similar circumstances would have been filled with sorrow. He said that 'sorrow is like furrows, the deeper they go, the more plentiful is the fruit we obtain'.[43]

23

In Minneapolis a Jewish Rabbi came to 'Abdu'l-Bahá with a request that He speak in his synagogue. Part of their conversation reveals the Master's radiant acquiescence in time of adversity.

'Abdu'l-Bahá began speaking to him by saying, 'I have come from your real country – Jerusalem. I have passed forty-five years of my life in Palestine; but I was in prison . . .'

'We are all in prison in this world,' responded the Rabbi.

'Yes, I was imprisoned in two prisons.'

The Rabbi commented 'that one prison was sufficient.'

'I was resigned even then, and was in utmost joy and happiness,' declared 'Abdu'l-Bahá.[44]

Prayerfulness

24

'Abdu'l-Bahá's prayerfulness aided Him to sustain an equanimity even in times of deep sorrow and dire anguish. His 'love for God was the ground and cause of an equanimity which no circumstance could shake and of an inner happiness which no adversity affected . . .'⁴⁵ To be sure, in times of severe stress – when Bahá'u'lláh was away in the wilderness of Sulaymáníyyih and again when the Master Himself was in grave danger in 'Akká due to false accusations brought against Him – 'Abdu'l-Bahá was known to pray, and perhaps also to chant, throughout an entire night. The death of His beloved Father, Bahá'u'lláh, made Him momentarily almost lifeless – but He rallied and was sustained by His abiding love of God. Indeed it is reported that the Master 'often prayed that His conditions might become more severe in order that His strength to meet them might be increased.'⁴⁶

25

'Abdu'l-Bahá sent a Tablet to an American believer in which He wrote: 'As to thy question, "Why pray? What is the wisdom thereof, for God has established everything and executes all affairs after the best order and He ordains everything according to a becoming measure and puts things in their places with the greatest propriety and perfection – therefore what is the wisdom in beseeching and supplicating and in stating one's wants and seeking help?" Know thou, verily, it is becoming of a weak one to supplicate to the strong One and it behoveth a seeker of bounty to beseech the glorious, bountiful One. When one supplicates to his Lord, turns to Him and seeks bounty from His ocean this supplication is by itself a light to his heart, an illumination to his sight, a life to his soul and an exaltation to his being.

'Therefore during thy supplications to God and thy reciting, "Thy name is my healing," consider how thy heart is cheered, thy soul delighted by the spirit of the love of God and thy mind attracted to the kingdom of

God! By these attractions one's ability and capacity increase. When the vessel is widened the water increaseth and when the thirst grows the bounty of the cloud becomes agreeable to the taste of man. This is the mystery of supplication and the wisdom of stating one's wants.'[47]

On the other hand, the Master also said, 'God will answer the prayer of every servant if that prayer is urgent.'[48]

26

To a correspondent, 'Abdu'l-Bahá wrote, 'Thou hast asked the wisdom of prayer. Know thou that prayer is indispensable and obligatory, and man under no pretext whatsoever is excused from performing the prayer unless he be mentally unsound, or an insurmountable obstacle prevent him. The wisdom of prayer is this: That it causeth a connection between the servant and the True One, because in that state [i.e., prayer] man with all heart and soul turneth his face towards His Highness the Almighty, seeking His association and desiring His love and compassion. The greatest happiness for a lover is to converse with his beloved, and the greatest gift for a seeker is to become familiar with the object of his longing; that is why with every soul who is attracted to the Kingdom of God, his greatest hope is to find an opportunity to entreat and supplicate before his Beloved, appeal for His mercy and grace and be immersed in the ocean of His utterance, goodness and generosity.

'Besides all this, prayer and fasting is the cause of awakening and mindfulness and conducive to protection and preservation from tests.'[49]

27

'When 'Abdu'l-Bahá was in New York, He called to Him an ardent Bahá'í and said, "If you will come to Me at dawn tomorrow, I will teach you to pray."

'Delighted, Mr M arose at four and crossed the city, arriving for his lesson at six. With what exultant expectation he must have greeted this opportunity! He found 'Abdu'l-Bahá already at prayer, kneeling by the side of the bed. Mr M followed suit, taking care to place himself directly across.

'Seeing that 'Abdu'l-Bahá was quite lost in His Own reverie, Mr M began to pray silently for his friends, his family and finally for the crowned heads of Europe. No word was uttered by the quiet Man before him. He went over all the prayers he knew then, and repeated them twice, three times – still no sound broke the expectant hush.

'Mr M surreptitiously rubbed one knee and wondered vaguely about his back. He began again, hearing as he did so, the birds heralding the dawn outside the window. An hour passed, and finally two. Mr M was quite numb now. His eyes, roving along the wall, caught sight of a large crack. He dallied with a touch of indignation but let his gaze pass again to the still figure across the bed.

'The ecstasy that he saw arrested him and he drank deeply of the sight. Suddenly he wanted to pray like that. Selfish desires were forgotten. Sorrow, conflict, and even his immediate surroundings were as if they had never been. He was conscious of only one thing, a passionate desire to draw near to God.

'Closing his eyes again he set the world firmly aside, and amazingly his heart teemed with prayer, eager, joyous, tumultuous prayer. He felt cleansed by humility and lifted by a new peace. 'Abdu'l-Bahá had taught him to pray!

'The "Master of 'Akká" immediately arose and came to him. His eyes rested smilingly upon the newly humbled Mr M. "When you pray," He said, "you must not think of your aching body, nor of the birds outside the window, nor of the cracks in the wall!"

'He became very serious then, and added, "When you wish to pray you must first know that you are standing in the presence of the Almighty!" '[50]

28

Once a friend asked the Master, 'How should one look forward to death?'

He replied, 'How does one look forward to the goal of any journey? With hope and with expectation. It is even so with the end of this earthly journey. In the next world, man will find himself freed from many of the disabilities under which he now suffers. Those who have passed on through death, have a sphere of their own. It is not removed from ours; their work, the work of the Kingdom, is ours; but it is sanctified from what we call "time and place". Time with us is measured by the sun. When there is no more sunrise, and no more sunset, that kind of time does not exist for man. Those who have ascended have different attributes from those who are still on earth, yet there is no real separation.

'In prayer there is a mingling of station, a mingling of condition. Pray for them as they pray for you!'[51]

'Abdu'l-Bahá as a young man

'Abdu'l-Bahá on His white donkey

29

One early pilgrim noted that grace was not said before meals. She mentioned this to the Master, to which He replied, 'My heart is in a continual state of thanksgiving, and so often those accustomed to this form say the words with the lips merely, and their hearts are far from being in a state of thanksgiving.'[52]

Yet, it is of interest that Thornton Chase, who is known as the first American believer, noted that 'Abdu'l-Bahá, always the perfect host, at the noon meal accepted food only after all those present had been served and then indicated that the meal should be eaten by saying 'In the Name of God'.

30

On one occasion the Master illustrated that prayer can be selfish. He told a story: 'It is said that once a Muhammedan, a Christian and a Jew were rowing in a boat. Suddenly a tempest arose and the boat was tossed on the crest of the waves and their lives were in danger. The Muhammedan began to pray: "O God! Drown this infidel of a Christian!" The Christian supplicated the Almighty: "O Father! Send to the bottom of the deep this Muslim!" They observed the Jew was not offering any prayer, and therefore asked him: "Why do you not pray for relief?" He answered, "I am praying. I am asking the Lord to answer the prayers of both of you!"'[53]

31

'Abdu'l-Bahá said, '. . . all effort and exertion put forth by man from the fullness of his heart is worship, if it is prompted by the highest motives and the will to do service to humanity. This is worship: to serve mankind and to minister to the needs of the people. Service is prayer.'[54]

Equanimity and Imperturbability

32

'Life at 'Akká and Haifa in the reign of 'Abdu'l-Ḥamíd was full of tension and danger. Palestine was a tinder box. Tribes fought each other. Crime was rampant. The streets of 'Akká were too narrow for bandits to roam free, but in Haifa they were a constant threat. Shots were heard every night but murderers were never apprehended. Whenever 'Abdu'l-Bahá was in Haifa, the Bahá'ís feared for His life and watched His movements. Frequently He went to visit the poor alone at night, refusing an escort or even a lantern-carrier. However, at a distance a Bahá'í would secretly watch His progress to the very door of His house.

'One night it was Yúnis Khán's turn to follow the Master. 'Abdu'l-Bahá was returning home past midnight when in the dark three shots rang out from a side street. Having become inured to the sound of gunfire, Yúnis Khán paid no attention to the first shot. The flash of the second shot sent him running toward the Master. He had reached the intersection when the third shot was fired and saw two men running away. He was now no more than a step behind the Master. 'Abdu'l-Bahá walked on without changing His pace or turning His head. His tread was firm and dignified. He had paid no attention to what had occurred but quietly murmured prayers as He walked. At the gate of His house He acknowledged Yúnis Khán's presence, turning to him and bidding him goodbye ('fí amáni'lláh' – under God's protection).'[55]

33

One of the most striking examples of 'Abdu'l-Bahá's imperturbability was His reaction to possible personal tragedy, further exile or execution. His troubles stemmed from the Covenant-breakers, those Bahá'ís who did not accept Bahá'u'lláh's Covenant with His followers that after His passing they should turn to 'Abdu'l-Bahá, the 'Most Great Branch', as the Head of the Bahá'í Faith and sole Interpreter of its teachings. These people wished that leadership for themselves and to that end were willing to bring astonishing and false accusations against 'Abdu'l-Bahá. Indeed they rumoured that the Master was building a fortress on Mount Carmel, where the Shrine of the Báb was prominently located on the side of the mountain. They even claimed He had raised an army of thirty thousand people in order to overthrow the Sulṭán ('Abdu'l-Ḥamíd) himself.

Given the instability existing in Turkey at that time, and the Sulṭán's fear of impending rebellion, a Commission of enquiry was appointed and 'Abdu'l-Bahá summoned to court. With courage He 'exposed the absurdity of these accusations, acquainted the members of the Commission, in support of His argument, with the provisions of Bahá'u'lláh's Testament, expressed His readiness to submit to any sentence the court might

decide to pass on Him, and eloquently affirmed that if
they should chain Him, drag Him through the streets,
execrate and ridicule Him, stone and spit upon Him,
suspend Him in the public square, and riddle Him with
bullets, He would regard it as a signal honor, inasmuch as
He would thereby be following in the footsteps, and
sharing the sufferings, of His beloved Leader, the Báb.'
The situation was so serious that pilgrimages were
temporarily suspended, mail handled in Egypt rather
than in Haifa and sacred Bahá'í Writings placed in safe
custody. Gatherings in 'Abdu'l-Bahá's home were cur-
tailed and spies constantly watched the Master's activities.

The Guardian wrote that, nevertheless, 'It was during
these troublous times, the most dramatic period of His
ministry, when, in the hey-day of His life and in the full
tide of His power, He, with inexhaustible energy,
marvelous serenity and unshakable confidence, initiated
and resistlessly prosecuted the varied enterprises associated with that ministry.'[56] It was during these years,
although still confined within the walls of the prison-city
of 'Akká, that, even at the height of His difficulties, He
never allowed work on the construction of the Shrine of
the Báb to be interrupted. Of His correspondence the
Guardian recorded: 'Eye-witnesses have testified that,
during that agitated and perilous period of His life, they
had known Him to pen, with His own Hand, no less than
ninety Tablets in a single day, and to pass many a night,
from dusk to dawn, alone in His bed-chamber engaged in
a correspondence which the pressure of His manifold
responsibilities had prevented Him from attending to in
the day-time.'[57] Reference to the account of this period
given by the Guardian in God Passes By (chapter XVII)
will give an idea of the amazing scope and variety of
'Abdu'l-Bahá's activities and achievements at this time.

'So imperturbable was 'Abdu'l-Bahá's equanimity

that, while rumors were being bruited about that He might be cast into the sea, or exiled to Fízán in Tripolitania, or hanged on the gallows, He, to the amazement of His friends and the amusement of His enemies, was to be seen planting trees and vines in the garden of His house, whose fruits when the storm had blown over, He would bid His faithful gardener, Ismá'íl Áqá, pluck and present to those same friends and enemies on the occasion of their visits to Him.'[58]

The Master knew what He was talking about when He wrote: '. . . O ye lovers of God, make firm your steps in His Cause, with such resolve that ye shall not be shaken though the direst of calamities assail the world. By nothing, under no conditions, be ye perturbed.'[59]

Courage

34

During this same period of danger and crisis the Spanish Consul put an Italian freighter at the disposal of 'Abdu'l-Bahá in order that He might escape during the night, but He refused to flee to safety, though the Bahá'ís begged Him to do so. Instead He sent a message to the ship's captain: 'The Báb did not run away; Bahá'u'lláh did not run away; I shall not run away . . .'[60] After three days and nights the freighter departed without the Master.

35

Later, in 1907, four members of a second Commission of investigation arrived by ship from Turkey. 'A few days before its arrival 'Abdu'l-Bahá had a dream, which He recounted to the believers, in which He saw a ship cast anchor off 'Akká, from which flew a few birds, resembling sticks of dynamite, and which, circling about His head, as He stood in the midst of a multitude of the frightened inhabitants of the city, returned without exploding to the ship.'[61]

The members of the Commission remained in 'Akká for approximately a month. They went to look at the stone edifice on the mountain. They asked 'Abdu'l-Bahá to appear before them. Now, He refused to do so. Furious, the chairman wanted an 'order from the Sulṭán to have Me hanged at the gate of 'Akká,' 'Abdu'l-Bahá later said in London.[62] The ship stood ready to carry 'Abdu'l-Bahá away with the Commission members. The Master remained calm and confident. He even told the believers who were yet in 'Akká, 'The meaning of the dream I dreamt is now clear and evident. Please God this dynamite will not explode.'[63]

Then, mysteriously, one day the Commission's ship began to leave the harbour in Haifa and move towards 'Akká. The Bahá'ís and family of the Master were filled with anguish on learning of this. They feared the Master would be taken aboard and carried away. Meanwhile, He was 'pacing, alone and silent, the courtyard of His house.'[64] But at dusk, wonder of wonders, the ship had obviously changed its direction. She was heading directly for Constantinople. There had been an attempt on the life of the Sulṭán. When the Commission submitted its report to him, it was not even considered, as the Sulṭán and his government were 'too preoccupied to consider the matter'. Some months later the 'Young Turk' Revolution of 1908 freed all political and religious prisoners of the old regime. This included 'Abdu'l-Bahá – free at last in 1908! In 1909 the Sulṭán himself was deposed.

36

While in Paris, 'Abdu'l-Bahá received a letter warning Him that if He visited a certain country, He would be in danger. When He heard of this, He smilingly remarked to Lady Blomfield, 'My daughter, have you not yet realized that never, in my life, have I been for one day out of danger, and that I should rejoice to leave this world and go to my Father?'

Lady Blomfield was 'overcome with sorrow and terror'. He continued, 'Be not troubled. These enemies have no power over my life, but that which is given them from on High. If my Beloved God so willed that my life-blood should be sacrificed in His path, it would be a glorious day, devoutly wished for by me.'[65]

Calm and Serenity

37

'Abdu'l-Bahá's love of God and Bahá'u'lláh brought a calm and a serenity which adverse circumstances could not shake, whether it be shots fired in the night, chains, locusts, bombardments of Haifa, or the threat of death. For example, He did not wish to conceal the chains with which He was 'paraded through the streets' accompanied by friendly soldiers.[66] In 1915 locusts destroyed the vegetation. For months news from the Bahá'í world did not reach Him and Haifa endured three bombardments. Lua Getsinger wrote that it was wonderful to witness the calm majesty of 'Abdu'l-Bahá as He went about among the people, whose only hope and help He was.[67]

38

'Abdu'l-Bahá did not permit the pressures of travel to
ruffle Him. Once while in Great Britain when it was time
to depart for a journey – secretaries and friends were
ready to leave for the train – He remained 'calmly
writing'. Reminded that it was time to leave, He quietly
replied, 'There are things of more importance than
trains.' He continued to write. 'Suddenly in breathless
haste a man came in, carrying in his hand a beautiful
garland of fragrant white flowers. Bowing low before
the Master, he said: "In the name of the disciples of
Zoroaster, The Pure One, I hail Thee as the 'Promised
Sháh Bahrám'!" ★

'Then the man, for a sign, garlanded 'Abdu'l-Bahá,
and proceeded to anoint each and all of the amazed
friends who were present with precious oil, which had
the odour of fresh roses.

'This brief but impressive ceremony concluded,
'Abdu'l-Bahá, having carefully divested Himself of the
garland, departed for the train.'[68]

39

One day in September 1912 'Abdu'l-Bahá left Chicago
for Kenosha. The party was scheduled to change trains *en
route* but, to the chagrin of His friends, He missed His
connection. However, He simply told them '. . . it
matters not. There is a wisdom in it.' They caught the
next train, only to find *en route* that the train they had

★ In fact, according to Bahá'í teachings, the 'Sháh Bahrám' promised by
Zoroaster was Bahá'u'lláh (see Shoghi Effendi, *God Passes By*, p. 94), not
'Abdu'l-Bahá, who made it abundantly clear that He was not a Manifestation
of God.

missed had been badly damaged in a collision with another train and passengers had been wounded. The Master was fully aware of the protection that had been theirs and told the friends that when He was departing from Alexandria on His way to America, the suggestion had been made that He should take the newly launched *Titanic* from London: it went down on that voyage. He affirmed that He had been guided to come by the direct route.[69]

40

Even during those crowded days in London the Master never appeared tense or frustrated, wondering how He could do all that seemed to be required of Him. He knew His purpose and thus all things fell into their proper perspective. Before He left London in 1913 at the close of His second visit, He gave a talk at Cadogan Gardens, clearly stating that teaching the Bahá'í Faith called for 'undivided attention'. 'Teach the Cause to those who do not know. It is now six months that Siyyid Asadu'lláh implored that I write a few lines to my sister, my daughters. I have not done this because I find I must teach. I enter all meetings, all churches, so that the Cause may be spread. When the "Most Important" work is before our sight, we must let go the "Important" one.'[70]

41

The calm with which 'Abdu'l-Bahá walked His 'chosen highway' endured until the very end of His earthly life. When He knew that His time had come He did not accept the food offered Him, saying, 'You wish me to take some food, and I am going?' He gave His two daughters 'a beautiful look. His face was so calm, his expression so serene, they thought him asleep.'[71]

Trust

42

The Master knew that God was at the helm. He needed only to move as His Captain wished. He put His affairs in God's hand and avoided the frustrations and the frenzy most mortals experience. An example of this was when the military commanders of Jerusalem and Damascus came to visit Him. Invited to the Holy City of Jerusalem, 'His answer to them was, "Inshallah" (If God is willing).'[72]

He was virtually never hurried, never harried. His plans were based upon 'God willing' – words He often used.

Submission

43

'Abdu'l-Bahá had occasion to try to comfort a woman who had lost her beloved baby over twenty-one years before. He asked her not to cry. He told her, 'I had a son who was four years old, and when he died I did not at all change My attitude. I gave My son to God as a trust, and so at his death I did not grieve.'[73]

Devotion

44

Stanwood Cobb, a Bahá'í educator, recalled his last interview with the Master in the United States. His heart was so full He could scarcely recall what was said. He knew he was embraced and three times 'Abdu'l-Bahá said, '*Be on fire with the love of the Kingdom!*' A little mystified by what these words actually meant, Mr Cobb knew that these nine precious words summed up the essence of 'Abdu'l-Bahá's Divine Teachings.[74]

45

Just before Mrs C left the household of 'Abdu'l-Bahá in 'Akká, 'He came into her room to say farewell, and seating Himself by the window looked off upon the sea in silence for so long a time that His guest began to wonder if He had forgotten her presence.

'Then at length He turned to her and said, with that eager speech that is one of His peculiarities: "Mrs C when you go back to New York talk to people about the love of God. People in the world do not talk enough about God. Their conversation is filled with trivialities, and they forget the most momentous subjects. Yet if you speak to them of God they are happy, and presently they open their hearts to you. Often you can not mention this glorious Revelation, for their prejudice would interfere, and they would not listen. But you will find that you can always talk to them about the love of God."

'Then He went away, and Mrs C sat a long time in the gathering darkness, while the glory of the sun descended upon the glittering waters of the Mediterranean. The fragrant shadows seemed to echo softly with the last words of 'Abdu'l-Bahá: "You will find that you can always talk to them about the love of God." '[75]

Contentment

Already as a child, the Master learned contentment. It was born of hardship. At a later time, He had good reason to write, regarding children, 'accustom them to hardship'.[76]

46

In Europe, on one occasion, remembering the desperate days in Ṭihrán when Bahá'u'lláh was incarcerated, their home sacked and their properties confiscated, 'Abdu'l-Bahá could yet say, 'Detachment does not imply lack of means; it is marked by the freedom of the heart. In Ṭihrán, we possessed everything at a nightfall, and on the morrow we were shorn of it all, to the extent that we had no food to eat. I was hungry, but there was no bread to be had. My mother poured some flour into the palm of my hand, and I ate that instead of bread. Yet, we were contented.'[77]

47

Prison walls themselves did not obscure the happiness in the heart of 'Abdu'l-Bahá. In prison He could write, 'Grieve not because of my imprisonment and calamity; for this prison is my beautiful garden, my mansioned paradise and my throne of dominion among mankind.

My calamity in my prison is a crown to me in which I glory among the righteous.'[78]

At another time He wrote, 'Anybody can be happy in the state of comfort, ease, health, success, pleasure and joy; but if one will be happy and contented in the time of trouble, hardship and prevailing disease, it is the proof of nobility.'[79]

It is a beautiful thing to realize that life's experiences did not sour or embitter the Master's outlook. Tuberculosis at the age of seven, poverty, exile, separation from Bahá'u'lláh, imprisonment, the death of His sons – He endured all these, and more, and remained optimistic and cheerful towards life. He walked nobly in adversity.

48

In His 'Will and Testament', written at a time of particular danger and difficulties, 'Abdu'l-Bahá turned to God in prayer: 'Thou seest me immersed in a sea of unsurpassed tribulation, sunk into a fathomless abyss, afflicted by mine enemies, and consumed with the flame of their hate, enkindled by my kinsmen with whom Thou didst make Thy strong Covenant and Thy firm Testament, wherein Thou biddest them turn their hearts to this wronged one . . .'[80]

And yet He could pray, 'Lowly, suppliant, and fallen upon my face, I beseech Thee with all the ardour of my invocation to pardon whosoever hath hurt me, forgive him that hath conspired against me and offended me, and wash away the misdeeds of them that have wrought injustice upon me. Vouchsafe unto them Thy goodly gifts, give them joy . . .'[81]

He truly could tell His friends that if others 'poison your lives, sweeten their souls . . .' He knew well that contentment and happiness must often be forged out of sorrow and grief.

It has already been amply shown that 'Abdu'l-Bahá did not seek an easy course through life. He accepted hard knocks graciously. He never flinched at that which was hard to accomplish. He performed work in the spirit of service, knowing it was deemed worship. Complaining was foreign to His nature. Contentment in the will of God was natural to His spirit.

49

One day 'a man passing by the gates of 'Abdu'l-Bahá's house in Haifa, carrying a basket, put it down as soon as he saw Him, saying that he could not find a porter and had to carry the basket himself. 'Abdu'l-Bahá remarked afterwards that a man should not feel ashamed of doing useful work.'[82]

50

' 'Abdu'l-Bahá used to come on foot two miles in the heat carrying flower-pots on His shoulders. He was an old, old man with white hair and white beard and He used to carry these flower-pots to the tomb of Bahá'u'lláh from one of the gardens in order to plant them near the tomb of His Father. There was a pump on the side of the wall of the tomb of Bahá'u'lláh in the old days, one of those hand-pumps that you have to handle. I heard that 'Abdu'l-Bahá used to stand, as an old man, and pump water until from standing against the wall and working He was so stiff He could not walk away from it. Once they had to come and lift Him away from the wall and rub His legs until the circulation came back. And they said "Why do you tire yourself so, 'Abdu'l-Bahá?" He said "What can I do for Bahá'u'lláh?"'[83] Rúḥíyyih <u>Kh</u>ánum spoke these words while on her travels in India.

51

The Master sometimes made His points through telling stories. Julia Grundy recorded the following story of His: 'A master had a slave who was completely devoted to him. One day he gave the slave a melon which when cut open looked most ripe and delicious. The slave ate one piece, then another and another with great relish (the day being warm) until nearly the whole melon had disappeared. The master, picking up the last slice, tasted it and found it exceedingly bitter and unpalatable. "Why, it is bitter! Did you not find it so?" he asked the servant. "Yes, my Master," the slave replied, "it was bitter and unpleasant, but I have tasted so much sweetness from thy hand that one bitter melon was not worth mentioning."'[84]

52

Once when 'Abdu'l-Bahá was out walking two ladies saw Him and asked to be introduced to Him. They then asked Him about the Faith. They thought He must be extremely wealthy and did not hesitate to tell Him so. He replied, 'My riches are of the Kingdom and not of this world. . . . Although I have nothing, yet I am richer than all the world.'[85]

Cheerfulness

The Master wanted people to be happy not only because then they could come to know the spiritual life, but also because in that condition they could make others happy too.[86]

Similarly He once told one of His daughters who was to travel with her aunt that she should be a cheerful companion.

53

Horace Holley, who became a well-known Bahá'í writer and administrator, came from Siena, in Italy, to see 'Abdu'l-Bahá when He was spending a little time at the Hôtel du Parc in Thonon-les-Bains on Lake Geneva in France. Mr Holley recalled one dinner: 'Our party took seats at two adjoining tables. The dinner was throughout cheerful and animated. 'Abdu'l-Bahá answered questions and made frequent observations on religion in the West. He laughed heartily from time to time – indeed, the idea of asceticism or useless misery of any kind cannot attach itself to this fully-developed personality. The divine element in Him does not feed at the expense of the human element, but appears rather to vitalize and enrich the human element by its own abundance, as if He had attained His spiritual development by fulfilling His social relations with the utmost ardour.'[87]

Laughter

'Abdu'l-Bahá loved laughter and His laughter was often a source of solace. One writer observed that once He laughed so heartily at the observations and questions directed to Him that 'His turban became disarranged. As He lifted His hands to straighten it, He smiled as though we had a little joke between us.'[88]

54

In London 'Abdu'l-Bahá had an interview with a representative from the *Weekly Budget*. He spoke of His first summer in 'Akká: ' 'Akká is a fever-ridden town. It was said that a bird attempting to fly over it would drop dead. The food was poor and insufficient, the water was drawn from a fever-infected well and the climate and conditions were such, that even the natives of the town fell ill. Many soldiers succumbed and eight out of ten of our guard died. During the intense heat, malaria, typhoid and dysentery attacked the prisoners, so that all, men, women and children, were sick at one time. There were no doctors, no medicines, no proper food, and no treatment of any kind.

'I used to make broth for the people, and as I had much practice, I make good broth,' the Master testified laughingly.[89]

55

There was a time when 'Abdu'l-Bahá was in chains. The jailers were amazed that the Master sang and laughed. He informed them they were doing Him a kindness – He had wanted to know the feelings of a man in chains. Now He knew![90]

56

One summer day a luncheon was held in Dublin, New Hampshire, in the home of Mrs Parsons who had 'asked some twenty people, all outstanding in various walks of life, to meet 'Abdu'l-Bahá. Culture, science, art, wealth, politics, achievement – all were represented.'[91] 'Most of those present at this luncheon party knew a little of 'Abdu'l-Bahá's life history, and, presumably, were expecting a dissertation from Him on the Bahá'í Cause. The hostess had suggested to the Master that He speak to them on the subject of Immortality. However, as the meal progressed, and no more than the usual common-places of polite society were mentioned, the hostess made an opening, as she thought, for 'Abdu'l-Bahá to speak on spiritual things.

'His response to this was to ask if He might tell them a story, and He related one of the Oriental tales, of which He had a great store and at its conclusion all laughed heartily.

'The ice was broken. Others added stories of which the Master's anecdote had reminded them. Then 'Abdu'l-Bahá, His face beaming with happiness, told another story, and another. His laughter rang through the room. He said that . . . It is good to laugh. Laughter is a spiritual relaxation. When they were in prison, He said, and under the utmost deprivation and difficulties, each of them at the close of the day would relate the most ludicrous event which had happened. Sometimes it was a little difficult to find one but always they would laugh until the tears would run down their cheeks. Happiness, He said, is never dependent upon material surroundings, otherwise how sad those years would have been. As it was they were always in the utmost state of joy and happiness.'

That was the nearest He came to talking about the Bahá'í message but the effect on those present was undoubtedly greater than any 'learned dissertation would have caused in them'.

'After the guests had gone, and 'Abdu'l-Bahá was leaving for His hotel, He came close to His hostess and asked her, with a little wistful smile, almost, she was used to say, like a child seeking approbation, if she were pleased with Him.'[92]

57

Dr J. E. Esslemont, author of the often-printed *Bahá'u'-lláh and the New Era*, was 'Abdu'l-Bahá's guest in Haifa for two and a half months in the winter of 1919–20. He observed, 'Both at lunch and supper He used to entertain a number of pilgrims and friends, and charm His guests with happy and humorous stories as well as precious talks on a great variety of subjects. "My home is the home of laughter and mirth," He declared, and indeed it was so. He delighted in gathering together people of various races, colours, nations, and religions in unity and cordial friendship around His hospitable board.'[93]

As He said on another occasion, 'My home is the home of peace. My home is the home of joy and delight. My home is the home of laughter and exultation. Whoever enters through the portals of this home must go out with gladsome heart.'[94]

58

Two ladies had an interview with 'Abdu'l-Bahá in New York City. Ella Quant wrote about that occasion: 'He told Margaret He prayed for her parents (who had passed into the life beyond some months before). Her eyes filled with tears and overflowed; mine then did likewise. The interpreter, perhaps at a loss, shook his head at us and said in an admonishing tone that we should never cry in His presence. It made Him sad. As I looked up, I saw that 'Abdu'l-Bahá's sadness was for us – not for Himself – for with hands outstretched to calm and protect us, like a mother bird hovering over her young in the nest, He exclaimed in English, *Laugh! Laugh!* I shall never forget that voice, vibrant and powerful beyond any words of mine to express. In that voice I have come to see the power of heaven to rout all negative forces of existence, and in arising to obey that command to find the eternal joy of life.'[95] The Master could call for laughter even at a time such as that – this need not seem strange when one realizes that He saw death as 'a messenger of joy'.

59

'An American friend who had enjoyed the privilege of more than one visit to 'Akká during the days of the exile of 'Abdu'l-Bahá, related an incident that took place at His table. With her sat persons of varied races, some of them traditional enemies who had now grown so to love one another that life and fortune would not have been too much to give, if called upon to do so. As the reality of their love gradually became plain to her, there was born a ray of the knowledge of the intimacy of the near ones in the world beyond. When the meal drew to a close,

'Abdu'l-Bahá spoke of the immortal worlds. As nearly as she could remember, the words He spoke were these: "We have sat together many times before, and we shall sit together many times again in the Kingdom. We shall laugh together very much in those times, and we shall tell of the things that befell us in the Path of God. In every world of God a new Lord's Supper is set for the faithful!" '96

Humour

'Abdu'l-Bahá was blessed with a delightful sense of humour. He found fun in situations and stories. A few examples will illustrate this.

60

'One day in the Holy Land He told Harlan Ober, an American Bahá'í, that he was to go to India. Harlan Ober did travel far and wide in the interests of the Faith, but at that particular time he did not cherish making that journey. A few days later 'Abdu'l-Bahá told him to go to America. "But, Master," Ober said, "I thought I was going to India." "So did Christopher Columbus," 'Abdu'l-Bahá replied.'97

61

Once a reporter in London inquired about 'Abdu'l-Bahá's plans – to his astonishment the Master replied in English. The reporter commented on His good pronunciation, whereupon 'Abdu'l-Bahá 'rose up and, pacing the room, uttered a number of complicated English words, such as "hippopotamus", and then laughingly said, "Very difficult English words I speak." '[98]

62

Lady Blomfield cited another instance of His delightful humour: 'One day after a meeting when, as usual, many people had crowded round Him, 'Abdu'l-Bahá arrived home very tired. We were sad at heart that He should be so fatigued, and bewailed the many steps to be ascended to the flat. Suddenly, to our amazement, the Master ran up the stairs to the top very quickly without stopping.

'He looked down at us as we walked up after Him, saying with a bright smile, from which all traces of fatigue had vanished: "You are all very old! I am very young!" ' He added, ' "Through the power of Bahá'u'-lláh all things can be done. I have just used that power." '[99]

63

As the Master travelled in the West, He compared the East and the West and was delighted with the contrasts.

In the Hotel Rittenhouse in Philadelphia about fifty people were crowded into a small room for a meeting with the Master. For lack of chairs some people sat on the floor – this delighted 'Abdu'l-Bahá. He commented, 'This is a cause of unity; see! The Occident is sitting on the floor like the Orient and the Orient is sitting on the chairs.' He laughed with delight and then gave His talk. [100]

64

One day in London 'Abdu'l-Bahá heard laughter coming from the kitchen. Delighted, He joined the happy people. 'It appeared that the Persian servant had remarked: "In the East women wear veils and do all the work." To which [the] English housekeeper had replied: "In the West women don't wear veils, and take good care that the men do at least some of the work. You had better get on with cleaning that silver."' The Master joined in the laughter.[101]

65

When, as the guest of Lady Blomfield, 'Abdu'l-Bahá 'sat down to dinner on Christmas eve, He said, playfully, that He was not hungry, but He had to come to the dinner table because Lady Blomfield was very insistent; two despotic monarchs of the East had not been able to command Him and bend His will, but the ladies of America and Europe, because they were free, gave Him orders.'[102]

66

In New York City a young supporter of tax-reform asked, 'What message shall I take to my friends?' The Master laughed with delighted humour: 'Tell them to come into the Kingdom of God. There they will find plenty of land – and there are no taxes on it!'[103]

67

In Edinburgh, 'Abdu'l-Bahá addressed the Esperantists. A serious advocate for the establishment of an international auxiliary language, He cited an anecdote to stress how important proper communication between people is: 'I recall an incident which occurred in Bagdad. There were two friends who knew not each other's language. One fell ill, the other visited him, but not being able to express his sympathy in words, resorted to gesture, as if to say, "How do you feel?" With another sign the sick [one] replied, "I shall soon be dead"; and his visitor, believing the gesture to indicate that he was getting better, said, "God be praised!"'[104]

68

'Abdu'l-Bahá told another story pointing out the necessity of one common language: 'At the city gate four travelers sat, a Persian, a Turk, an Arab and a Greek. They were hungry and wanted their evening meal. So one was selected to buy for them all. But among them they could not agree as to what should be bought. The Persian said angoor, the Turk uzum, the Arab wanted aneb and the Greek clamored for staphylion, green and black. They quarrelled and wrangled and almost came to blows in trying to prove that the particular desire of each was the right food. When all of a sudden there passed a donkey ladened with grapes. Each man sprang to his feet and with eager hands pointed out: "See uzum!" said the Turk. "See aneb!" said the Arab. "See angoor!" said the Persian. And the Greek said, "See staphylion!" Then they bought their grapes and were at peace.'[105]

69

On the train from Sacramento to Denver, 'a salesman came through the cars selling pennants of various schools.' The Master joked, 'Tell him to bring the banner of universal peace if he has it. We want a flag under which the whole world may find rest and peace.' Other passengers heard 'Abdu'l-Bahá and formed a group in the corridor in order to be able to talk with Him.[106]

EPILOGUE

The Effect of 'Abdu'l-Bahá's Words and Deeds

I

One writer reported that 'Abdu'l-Bahá once compared the Bahá'í Faith to a garden. In essence He said, 'At the gate of the garden some stand and look within, but do not care to enter. Others step inside, behold its beauty, but do not penetrate far. Still others encircle this garden inhaling the fragrance of the flowers and, having enjoyed its full beauty, pass out again by the same gate. But there are always some who enter and, becoming intoxicated with the splendor of what they behold, remain for life to tend the garden.'[1] 'Abdu'l-Bahá opened the gate to the garden of God and led the way for all who wished to follow. Surely no mortal can ever judge the total effect of 'Abdu'l-Bahá's exemplary life on a multitude of others – Bahá'ís, as well as on friend and foe alike.

Once Bahá'u'lláh turned to 'Alí Muḥammad Varqá, saying, 'See 'Abdu'l-Bahá, the Master, what a wonderful effect His deeds and words have in the world! See how kindly and patiently He endures every difficulty.'[2]

Many were those who paid tribute to 'Abdu'l-Bahá. Juliet Thompson, His devoted disciple, wrote, 'As He walked among the people, an Immortal in a less than human world, with His ineffable beauty, His scintillating power, His strange, unearthly majesty, eyes full of wonder followed Him.

'The poet, Kahlil Gibran, said: "For the first time I saw form noble enough to be the receptacle for [the] Holy Spirit!"

'An atheist went to a church to hear Him speak and

later eagerly sought Him at His house. When this atheist was asked: "Did you feel the greatness of 'Abdu'l-Bahá?" he indignantly replied: "Would you feel the greatness of Niagara?"

'Those who met Him perceived no more than their capacity could register. A society woman exclaimed: "Such beauty – the beauty of strength! And such charm! Why, He is a perfect man of the world!" And another society woman who had talked at length with Him: "You can hide nothing from Him! He looked into my heart and discovered all its secrets."

'A woman in sorrow, passing through a cruel experience, said: "He took all the bitterness out of my heart." A famous playwright, when he came from the room of 'Abdu'l-Bahá, declared: "I have been in the presence of God!" 'And Lee McClung, then Treasurer of the United States, after his meeting with the Master, groping for words to describe the experience, said: ' "I felt as if I were in the presence of a great Prophet – Isaiah – Elijah – no, that is not it. The presence of Christ – no. I felt as if I were in the presence of my Divine Father.'

'The Turkish ambassador, Zia Pasha, a devout Muhammadan, when told of the advent of Bahá'u'lláh, had scoffed at the thought of a new Prophet. But while 'Abdu'l-Bahá was in Washington Zia Pasha met Him at the Persian Embassy, invited by His Excellency Ali-Kuli Khan, and Madame Khan, and immediately arranged a dinner to be given in His honor at the Turkish Embassy. At this dinner the ambassador rose and, facing 'Abdu'l-Bahá with tears in his eyes, toasted Him as "The Light of the age, Who has come to spread His glory and perfection among us." '3

Juliet Thompson, an artist, left vivid word-pictures as she saw Him in the West: 'Abdu'l-Bahá with the power of his peace in the restless West; 'Abdu'l-Bahá in the complex West with the power of his simplicity; 'Abdu'l-

Bahá with his noble and illumined beauty in the artificial and skeptical West; – so strongly defined in his completeness against our undevelopment!

'And that illumined beauty – that dignity, not of this world – that majesty of spirit that marks him a king among men, never went unheeded; for wherever he passed, eyes turned to follow, and the crowds with involuntary reverence, stood back.'[4]

At one time a Syrian woman in Boston pushed aside the crowd which had gathered around the Master, fell to His feet and exclaimed, 'I confess that in Thee I have recognized the Spirit of God and Jesus Christ Himself'.[5]

Lady Blomfield reported, 'A doctor, who had been in Alexandria, where he saw 'Abdu'l-Bahá and witnessed His Christ-like life, told me that for the *first* time he was able to understand what the Lord Christ must have been like. "*Now* I am able to believe," he said.'[6]

A Swiss lady, viewing the picture of the Master for the first time, 'caught it up in her hands crying: "*Oh! c'est le visage du Bon Dieu!*"* and shed tears.'[7] 'Abdu'l-Bahá, of course, was neither God Himself nor His Prophet – He never made such claims. His station was unique – He was the 'Mystery of God' – and people felt in Him something extraordinary.

2

Undoubtedly, one of the most extraordinary gatherings with the Master on His vast transcontinental trip in America in 1912 occurred at Palo Alto, California. Here, at Leland Stanford Junior University, almost two thousand students and staff crowded into an assembly hall to hear this wise Man from the Orient.

---

* 'Oh! It is the face of the (good) Lord!'

Unity Feast given by 'Abdu'l-Bahá on 29 June 1912, at West Englewood, New Jersey

'Abdu'l-Bahá signing a Tablet outside His
house in Haifa

Dr David Starr Jordan, scientist, pragmatist, one-time teacher of Herbert Hoover and first president of this now great university, extended to 'Abdu'l-Bahá a hospitality which gave birth to one of the outstanding lectures the Master delivered while travelling in this country. Dr Jordan, who is credited with having said that ''Abdu'l-Bahá will surely unite the East and the West: for He treads the mystic way with practical feet,'[8] introduced the Speaker to that wide audience: 'It is our portion to have with us . . . one of the great religious teachers of the world, one of the natural successors of the old Hebrew Prophets . . . I have now the great pleasure and the great honor also of presenting to you 'Abdu'l-Bahá.' 'Abdu'l-Bahá stepped forward and delivered a masterful speech, suited to the audience and the times.[9]

Later the *Palo Altan* of 1 November headlined this unique occasion across an entire page. Mistaking 'Abdu'l-Bahá for a 'venerable prophet with His long gray beard and Persian cloak and turban', it said ''Abdu'l-Bahá carries the message of religion and Dr Jordan carries the message of science, both aiming for one great result. As all men are the children of one God so are they all brothers and we are at the dawning of a new day when the relationship of world fraternity will be seen and recognized . . .'[10]

3

The founder of Esperanto, Ludwig Zamenhof, remarked, 'I highly esteem the personality of 'Abdu'l-Bahá and his work. In him I see one of the greatest benefactors that humanity has produced.'[11]

4

In the Introduction to *A Traveller's Narrative*, translated into English from Persian by Edward G. Browne of the University of Cambridge, we read, concerning 'Abdu'l-Bahá: 'One more eloquent of speech, more ready of argument, more apt of illustration, more intimately acquainted with the sacred books of the Jews, the Christians, and the Muhammadans, could, I should think, scarcely be found even amongst the eloquent, ready, and subtle race to which he belongs. These qualities, combined with a bearing at once majestic and genial, made me cease to wonder at the influence and esteem which he enjoyed even beyond the circle of his father's followers. About the greatness of this man and his power no one who had seen him could entertain a doubt.'[12]

5

Prince Muḥammad-'Alí Páshá of Egypt commented, 'I considered Him the most important man in our century. A man like 'Abbás Bábá cannot be replaced, that is my opinion. He had such a great spirit, such a powerful brain and such a grasp of realities!'[13]

6

'Abdu'l-Bahá's photograph, alone, had a powerful influence on a little girl. There was that 'extraordinary experience of a woman whose little girl, as the result of a dream she had had, insisted that Jesus Christ was in the world, and who, at the sight of 'Abdu'l-Bahá's picture exposed in the window of a magazine store, had instantly identified it as that of the Jesus Christ of her dream – an act which impelled her mother, after reading that 'Abdu'l-Bahá was in Paris, to take the next boat for Europe and hasten to attain His presence . . .'[14]

7

Even thieves were influenced by the Master. In 1972, Margaret Ruhe wrote to me from Haifa that dear, old Mr Avron had recently come on pilgrimage from Persia – he had been on pilgrimage in Palestine for fifty-seven days in 1919. He was in the first group invited to come after the cessation of World War I. The journey from Ṭihrán took him three months then – moving by trains and boats and finally by carriage. Friends in Istanbul gave him silver pieces to bring as a gift to the Master in Haifa, but when they passed through 'Akká, they were accosted by thieves who tore open all their luggage, and stole many things. As they took the silver, Mr Avron said, 'That silver is for 'Abdu'l-Bahá.' Suddenly the thieves grew quiet; they said, ' 'Abdu'l-Bahá fed us; He clothed us, and housed us. Here is your silver for 'Abdu'l-Bahá.' Said Margaret Ruhe, 'We are reminded that 'Abdu'l-Bahá lived in 'Akká for over 40 years and was the outstanding citizen of that town and was the great Social Worker who served the people in countless ways day and night for endless years.'[15]

8

On one occasion Florence Khánum saw the Master when He 'raised His beloved face, and gazed upward lingeringly at the glory of the full moon. I can never forget those moments of beauty – the moon, a masterpiece of God, shining in full glory in the high heavens, being admiringly looked upon by a masterpiece of God on earth: 'Abdu'l-Bahá!'[16]

9

Louise Waite wrote: 'Once having accepted 'Abdu'l-Bahá's station, it is as useless to vex our minds with all these "whys and wherefores" as it would be for a way-worn traveler when a wagon comes along and the driver offers to carry him to town and he gladly climbs in, to continue to carry his heavy burden on his back. At 'Akká, I not only climbed into the wagon of Truth, but I also left my heavy bundle of self, opinions and perplexity of ideas by the roadside, knowing that this Divine Driver would carry me safely to town. God has indeed given us an "Ark of Safety" in 'Abdu'l-Bahá.

' 'Abdu'l-Bahá, the Mystery of God!

'Who can comprehend that Mystery? Surely not finite mind nor intellect. Only *through the heart* can we catch a faint glimpse of His Station.'[17]

10

Horace Holley, who later served as secretary of the National Spiritual Assembly of the Bahá'ís of the United States for many years, recalled his first sight of the

Master. People were seated at outdoor tables at a hotel at Thonon-les-Bains in France, on Lake Geneva. Others were strolling under the trees; an orchestra was playing. All this did not matter. Horace Holley, strong of intellect and not prone to show his emotions, was deeply stirred. Later that year he wrote, '. . . I saw among them a stately old man, robed in a cream-coloured gown, His white hair and beard shining in the sun. He displayed a beauty of stature, an inevitable harmony of attitude and dress I had never seen nor thought of in men. Without having ever visualized the Master, I knew that this was He. My whole body underwent a shock. My heart leaped, my knees weakened, a thrill of acute, receptive feeling flowed from head to foot. I seemed to have turned into some most sensitive sense-organ, as if eyes and ears were not enough for this sublime impression. In every part of me I stood aware of 'Abdu'l-Bahá's presence. From sheer happiness I wanted to cry – it seemed the most suitable form of self-expression at my command. While my own personality was flowing away, a new being, not my own assumed its place. A glory, as it were from the summits of human nature poured into me, and I was conscious of a most intense impulse to admire. In 'Abdu'l-Bahá I felt the awful presence of Bahá'u'lláh, and, as my thoughts returned to activity, I realized that I had thus drawn as near as man now may to pure spirit and pure being. This wonderful experience came to me beyond my own volition. I had entered the Master's presence and become the servant of a higher will for its own purpose. Even my memory of that temporary change of being bears strange authority over me. I *know* what men can become; and that single overcharged moment, shining out from the dark mountain-mass of all past time, reflects like a mirror I can turn upon all circumstances to consider their worth by an intelligence purer than my own.'[18]

II

When George Townshend read the words of 'Abdu'l-Bahá in one or two pamphlets which had reached him from America, he confessed, 'When I looked at those, that was the beginning and the end with me.'[19]

I2

The Master once said to Ida Boulter Slater: ' "You have sought the Kingdom of God in many places, and it was good, but now – you have arrived at home." And her reaction was: "I knew I had come home when I entered the Presence of 'Abdu'l-Bahá." '[20]

I3

A vivid and precious story of how one seeker's life was changed after he met the Master Teacher, 'Abdu'l-Bahá, comes to us through the pen of Howard Colby Ives, whose *Portals to Freedom* is a treasured book among Bahá'ís. A Unitarian minister, forty-six years of age, Ives knew that unhappiness which comes when the soul searches for God, yet seeks in vain. He loved Jesus and His Teachings – but how few real Christians were to be found! Although a successful minister with a good salary, these things did not really satisfy.

One day he found an article in *Everybody's Magazine* about 'Abdu'l-Bahá – a Man who had found a great truth and who – wonder of wonders! – never took up a collection when doing God's work. Eager to be of service to humanity, Mr Ives, in addition to preaching in a Unitarian church, had founded The Brotherhood

Church in Jersey City. On the Board of Trustees was a most lovable man, humble and sweet. This friend put him in touch with the Bahá'ís in New York City. When Mr Ives received an invitation to a Bahá'í meeting, he felt he owed it to his friend to investigate. At the meeting, instead of the usual 'religious trappings', he found an irresistible spirit. He felt he must get one of these Bahá'í speakers to his Brotherhood Church and this he did. Three remarkable months followed. He was particularly stirred by *The Seven Valleys* of Bahá'u'lláh. When 'Abdu'l-Bahá came to this country, he wanted an interview with Him – all alone – without even the benefit of an interpreter. To his utter amazement, this actually happened – and in their silence, the Master looked at him and it was as if no one had ever before really seen him. Here was a meeting of souls, with such an understanding and heartfelt love that the writer was literally moved to tears; tears which 'Abdu'l-Bahá lovingly wiped away. The Master told him that one must ever be happy, whereupon He laughed in a boyish fashion. Life was never again the same for Mr Ives.

In the weeks which followed 'Abdu'l-Bahá's arrival in the United States of America in 1912, Mr Ives was drawn to Him as a bee is drawn to honey. In retrospect, his temerity, as he went in pursuit of this magnetic Personality, so full of divine wisdom, astonished him. He felt impelled to be in the glowing presence of One who seemed always to be saying – but with infinite love – 'Come up higher!'[21] Once he followed 'Abdu'l-Bahá up the stairs to His room, the hour quite late, and knocked at His door. The Master Himself appeared. Howard Ives then asked, 'Will you please pray with me?' And then he recalled, 'He motioned, and I knelt while He put His hands upon my head and chanted, in Persian, a brief prayer. It was all over within three minutes. But those moments brought to me a peace I had never known.'[22]

Howard Ives observed well and learned fast. He became a life-long follower of 'Abdu'l-Bahá. He followed Him to the S.S. *Celtic* in New York that 5 December in 1912 when the Master sailed away. Once he had wondered about renunciation. He had heard the Master say that 'This is a Day for very great things – *very great things.*' Before long he gave up all denominational work to become a Bahá'í.

Then, one day in 1921, he and his wife, Mabel, made a great decision. She recalled, 'Our plan had been to earn a lot of money rapidly – enough to make us independent so we could give the rest of our lives to spreading the Cause. This proved to be a chimera, and our dream of traveling and teaching was no nearer fulfillment. Then one day we realized that we might go on the rest of our lives trying to establish security so that we might go out in the teaching field, but never do anything but simply work and dream of this future. So we decided that, because it was *utterly impossible* and *couldn't* be done, as we had no money, we would now go out and teach.

'So began our long Odyssey. We advertised for some selling proposition for two salesmen who wished to travel, received 21 answers, chose one, and felt ready to go. We sold or gave away all our earthly possessions, reduced all our earthly goods to a trunk or two and a couple of suitcases. When we had bought our train ticket to Pittsburgh, we had just $7.00 between us.'[23]

Mr Ives only began to write in 1934 at the age of sixty-seven. Before long his eyesight, along with his health, failed noticeably, but he wanted to record his 'spiritual memoirs', and *Portals to Freedom* was begun. When he was forbidden the use of his eyes, he still was undaunted . . . 'he learned the touch system on the typewriter and completed the book.'[24]

14

'When 'Abdu'l-Bahá came to America, H. S. Fugeta was a medical student at the University of Michigan. Like his famous forerunner who was short of stature, he climbed a sycamore tree to see the Master pass by. "Come down, Zachias, for this day I would sup with thee," called the flute-like voice of 'Abdu'l-Bahá, and Fugeta relinquishing every human tie followed Him back to Mount Carmel to become a helper in the household.'[25] Fujita, who passed away quite recently, spent most of his time, since that day in 1912, in the Holy Land.

15

Dorothy Baker became a Hand of the Cause of God. But '. . . in 1912 Mother Beecher [Dorothy's grandmother] took Dorothy, then fourteen years old, to New York to see 'Abdu'l-Bahá. She had been a very shy child, sensitive to the point of deep suffering in the presence of adults. She was so shy that years later she still remembered the tension she felt when she entered the room where 'Abdu'l-Bahá was speaking. He smiled at her, and without speaking to her directly, motioned her to a foot-stool at His side. At first she was so much afraid that He might speak to her that she could hardly bear it, but as He seemed to pay no further attention to her, she gradually relaxed. She was never able to remember what He talked about that day, but it was the moment of her birth as a Bahá'í, and from that time on she considered herself a Bahá'í. Although she left without speaking to Him, she could think of nothing else for days afterward and finally wrote Him a letter saying that she wished to serve the Faith.'[26] She developed into an outstanding and very effective Bahá'í speaker.

16

Carole Lombard Gable became a famous actress. Her Bahá'í teacher wrote, ' "The Carole who longed to meet and know her Lord, 'Abdu'l-Bahá, the Carole who planned to see Him, the Carole who spoke with the writer of the service she wanted to render her Lord – this Carole few people knew." Carole attended Mrs Lewis' classes held in Mrs Peters' [her mother's] home; at fourteen she wrote to the Master of her love for Him, her ambitions and longings, and she said, "If only He approves, I shall not fail." His Tablet came, praying for her success. Mrs Lewis writes, "Carole never failed to give credit to her Lord." ' Both she and her mother became Bahá'ís 'because of their great love for 'Abdu'l-Bahá'.[27]

17

On the fortieth day after the Master's passing, when an outstanding memorial feast was held, the Governor of Phoenicia, speaking to the hundreds of guests, said, 'Most of us here have, I think, a clear picture of Sir 'Abdu'l-Bahá 'Abbás, of His dignified figure walking thoughtfully in our streets, of His courteous and gracious manner, of His kindness, of His love for little children and flowers, of His generosity and care for the poor and suffering. So gentle was He, and so simple, that in His presence one almost forgot that He was also a great teacher, and that His writings and His conversations have been a solace and an inspiration to hundreds and thousands of people in the East and in the West.'[28]

18

'One of the distinguished figures in the academic life of the University of Oxford, a famous professor and scholar, wrote on behalf of himself and his wife: "The passing beyond the veil into fuller life must be specially wonderful and blessed for One Who has always fixed His thoughts on high, and striven to lead an exalted life here below." '[29]

19

E. G. Browne wrote for the January 1922 issue of the *Journal of the Royal Asiatic Society*, 'The death of 'Abbás Effendi, better known since he succeeded his father, Bahá'u'lláh, thirty years ago as 'Abdu'l-Bahá, deprives Persia of one of the most notable of her children and the East of a remarkable personality, who has probably exercised a greater influence not only in the Orient but in the Occident than any Asiatic thinker and teacher of recent times. . . . One of the most notable practical results of the Bahá'í ethical teaching in the United States has been, according to the recent testimony of an impartial and qualified observer, the establishment in Bahá'í circles in New York of a real fraternity between black and white, and an unprecedented lifting of the "colour bar", described by the said observer as "almost miraculous". '[30]

20

Dowager Queen Marie of Romania was one of many who found a deep happiness in the Message for a new day. In a letter to Shoghi Effendi she stated that, 'Indeed a great light came to me with the message of Bahá'u'lláh and 'Abdu'l-Bahá. It came as all great messages come at an hour of dire grief and inner conflict and distress, so the seed sank deeply.'

Also, in a statement in the *Toronto Daily Star* of 4 May 1926, she stated, 'Their writings are a great cry toward peace, reaching beyond all limits of frontiers, above all dissension about rites and dogmas. It is a religion based upon the inner spirit of God, upon the great, not-to-be-overcome verity that God is love, meaning just that. It teaches that all hatreds, intrigues, suspicions, evil words, all aggressive patriotism even, are outside the one essential law of God, and that special beliefs are but surface things whereas the heart that beats with divine love knows no tribe nor race.

'It is a wondrous Message that Bahá'u'lláh and his son 'Abdu'l-Bahá have given us. They have not set it up aggressively, knowing that the germ of eternal truth which lies at its core cannot but take root and spread.

'There is only one great verity in it: Love, the mainspring of every energy, tolerance toward each other, desire of understanding each other, knowing each other, helping each other, forgiving each other.

'It is Christ's Message taken up anew, in the same words almost, but adapted to the thousand years and more difference that lies between the year one and today. No man could fail to be better because of this Book.

'I commend it to you all. If ever the name of Bahá'u'lláh or 'Abdu'l-Bahá comes to your attention, do not put their writings from you. Search out their Books, and let their glorious, peace-bringing, love-creating words and lessons sink into your hearts as they have into mine . . . Seek them, and be the happier.'[31]

Queen Marie stated that the Bahá'í teaching 'is like a wide embrace gathering together all those who have long searched for words of hope.'[32]

21

What 'Abdu'l-Bahá's friends said of Him is inspiring. His life, His words and deeds have already had a profound effect upon countless thousands who were blessed to hear and to see Him. The Master's influence will be felt by unborn millions as His soul-stirring life touches their hearts. They, too, will strive to be as He was and they will cherish, as do we, the divine love story, *An Early Pilgrimage*, in which May Bolles (Maxwell) lovingly quoted 'Abdu'l-Bahá: 'Pray that your hearts may be cut from yourselves and from the world, that you may be confirmed by the Holy Spirit and filled with the fire of the love of God.'[33] '. . . I say unto you that anyone who will rise up in the Cause of God at this time shall be filled with the spirit of God, and that He will send His hosts from heaven to help you, and that nothing shall be impossible to you if you have faith. And now I give you a commandment which shall be for a covenant between you and Me – that ye have faith; that your faith be steadfast as a rock that no storms can move, that nothing can disturb, and that it endure through all things even to the end. . . . As ye have faith so shall your powers and blessings be. This is the balance – this is the balance – this is the balance.'[34]

'Another commandment I give unto you, that ye love one another even as I love you. Great mercy and blessings are promised to the people of your land, but on one condition: that their hearts are filled with the fire of love, that they live in perfect kindness and harmony like one soul in different bodies. If they fail in this condition the great blessings will be deferred. Never forget this; look at one another with the eye of perfection; look at Me, follow Me, be as I am; take no thought for yourselves or your lives, whether ye eat or whether ye sleep, whether ye are comfortable, whether ye are well or ill, whether ye are with friends or foes, whether ye receive praise or blame; for all of these things ye must care not at all. Look at Me and be as I am; ye must die to yourselves and to the world, so shall ye be born again and enter the Kingdom of Heaven. Behold a candle how it gives its light. It weeps its life away drop by drop in order to give forth its flame of light.'[35]

BIBLIOGRAPHY

'Abdu'l-Bahá. *'Abdu'l-Bahá in Canada*. Toronto, Ontario, Canada: National Spiritual Assembly of the Bahá'ís of Canada, 1962.

—— *Abdul Baha in London*. Addresses and Notes of Conversations. Chicago: Baha'i Publishing Society, 1921.

—— *Messages from Abdul Baha to the Honolulu Bahais*. Honolulu: National Spiritual Assembly of the Bahá'ís of the Hawaiian Islands (no date).

—— *Paris Talks*. London: Bahá'í Publishing Trust, 11th edn 1969.

—— *Promulgation of Universal Peace, The*. Discourses by Abdul Baha Abbas During His Visit to the United States in 1912. vol. I, Chicago: Executive Board of Baha'i Temple Unity, 1922. vol. II, Chicago: Baha'i Publishing Committee, 1925.

—— *Secret of Divine Civilization, The*. Wilmette, Illinois: Bahá'í Publishing Trust, 1957.

—— *Selections from the Writings of 'Abdu'l-Bahá*. Compiled by the Research Department of the Universal House of Justice. Haifa: Bahá'í World Centre, 1978.

—— *Some Answered Questions*. Wilmette, Illinois: Bahá'í Publishing Trust, 1981.

—— *Tablets of Abdul-Baha Abbas*. vol. I, New York: Baha'i Publishing Committee, second printing, July 1930. vol. II, Chicago: Baha'i Publishing Society, 1915. vol. III, New York: Baha'i Publishing Committee, second printing 1930.

—— *Tablets of the Divine Plan*. Wilmette, Illinois: Bahá'í Publishing Trust, 1959.

—— *Will and Testament of 'Abdu'l-Bahá*. New York: Bahá'í Publishing Committee, 1935. Also *Bahá'í World Faith* (see listing below).

Austin, Elsie. *Above All Barriers: The Story of Louis G. Gregory*. Wilmette, Illinois: Bahá'í Publishing Trust, 1976.

Bahá'í News (USA). National Spiritual Assembly of the Bahá'ís of the United States, Aug. 1962, Sept. 1970, Apr. 1973, Feb. 1974, Sept. 1977.

Bahá'í Prayers. A selection. London: Bahá'í Publishing Trust, rev. edn 1975.

Bahá'í Scriptures. A selection from the Bahá'í Holy Writings. New York: Bahá'í Publishing Committee, 2nd edn 1928.

Bahá'í World, The. vol. II, 1926–8. New York: Bahá'í Publishing Committee, 1928. vol. IV, 1930–2. New York: Bahá'í Publishing Committee, 1933. vol. VI, 1934–6. New York: Bahá'í Publishing Committee, 1937. vol. IX, 1940–4. Wilmette, Illinois: Bahá'í Publishing Committee, 1945. vol. XI, 1946–50. Wilmette, Illinois: Bahá'í Publishing Committee, 1952. vol. XII, 1950–4. Wilmette, Illinois: Bahá'í Publishing Trust, 1956. vol. XIII, 1954–63. Haifa, Israel: The Universal House of Justice, 1970.

Bahá'í World Faith. A selection from the Bahá'í Holy Writings. Wilmette, Illinois: Bahá'í Publishing Trust, 1976.

Bahá'u'lláh. *Gleanings from the Writings of Bahá'u'lláh*. Wilmette, Illinois: Bahá'í Publishing Trust, 1976.

—— *The Hidden Words of Bahá'u'lláh*. Wilmette, Illinois: Bahá'í Publishing Trust, 1982.

Baker, Dorothy. *The Path to God*. New York: Bahá'í Publishing Committee, 1937.

Balyuzi, H. M. *'Abdu'l-Bahá, The Centre of the Covenant of Bahá'u'lláh*. Oxford: George Ronald, 1973.

✓—— *Edward Granville Browne and the Bahá'í Faith*. Oxford: George Ronald, 1980.

Blomfield, Lady (Sitárih Khánum). *The Chosen Highway*. Wilmette, Illinois: Bahá'í Publishing Trust, 1967.

Blomfield, Lady and Shoghi Effendi. *The Passing of 'Abdu'l-Bahá*. Stuttgart: 1922.

Brown, Ramona Allen. *Memories of 'Abdu'l-Bahá*. Wilmette, Illinois: Bahá'í Publishing Trust, 1980.

Chase, Thornton. *In Galilee*. Chicago: Baha'i Publishing Society, 1921.

Child's Way. July–Aug. 1973. Now published by an editorial committee of the National Spiritual Assembly of the Bahá'ís of the United States.

Cobb, Stanwood. *Memories of Abdu'l-Bahá*. Washington, D.C.: Avalon Press (no date). Reprinted from *Bahá'í News*, July and Aug. 1962.

Compilation on Bahá'í Education, A. Compiled by the Research Department of the Universal House of Justice. Oakham, England: Bahá'í Publishing Trust, 1976.

Divine Art of Living, The. Compiled by Mabel Hyde Paine. Wilmette, Illinois: Bahá'í Publishing Trust, 1960.

Esslemont, J. E. *Bahá'u'lláh and the New Era*. Wilmette, Illinois: Bahá'í Publishing Trust, 1976.

Faizí, Abu'l-Qásim. *Milly – A Tribute to Amelia E. Collins*. Oxford: George Ronald, 1977.

Faizi, Gloria. *The Bahá'í Faith – An Introduction*. Lebanon: 1971.

Fathea'zam, Hooshmand. *The New Garden*. New Delhi, India: Bahá'í Publishing Trust, 5th edn 1971.

Ferraby, John. *All Things Made New*. A Comprehensive Outline of the Bahá'í Faith. London: Bahá'í Publishing Trust, 1975.

Ford, Bahíyyih. 'Notes of Bahíyyih Ford' (unpublished).

Ford, Mary Hanford. *The Oriental Rose*. New York: Broadway Publishing Co., 1910.

Gail, Marzieh. *The Sheltering Branch*. Oxford: George Ronald, 1978.

Garden of the Heart, The. Compiled from the Writings of Bahá'u'lláh and 'Abdu'l-Bahá by Frances Esty. Buffalo, New York: 1930.

Goodall, Helen S. and Cooper, Ella Goodall. *Daily Lessons Received at Acca January, 1908*. Chicago: Bahai Publishing Society, 1908.

Grundy, Julia M. *Ten Days in the Light of 'Akká*. Wilmette, Illinois: Bahá'í Publishing Trust, 1979.

Haney, Charles and Mariam. *A Heavenly Feast*. Some Utterances of Abdul-Baha. 1909 (no details).

Hofman, David. *The Renewal of Civilization*. Oxford: George Ronald, rev. edn 1969.

Holley, Horace. *Religion for Mankind*. Oxford: George Ronald, 1976.

Ives, Howard Colby. *Portals to Freedom*. Oxford: George Ronald, 1976.

Jordan, Daniel C. *The Meaning of Deepening*. Wilmette, Illinois: Bahá'í Publishing Trust, 1973.

Lucas, Mary. *A Brief Account of My Visit to Acca*. Chicago: Baha'i Publishing Society, 1905.

McDaniel, Allen Boyer. *The Spell of the Temple*. New York: Vantage Press, Inc., 1953.

Magazine of the Children of the Kingdom, The. Article by Ella M. Robarts. June 1924, vol. V. no. 3. Boston, Mass.

Mathews, Loulie Albee. *Not Every Sea Hath Pearls*. Portsmouth, Hampshire: Loulie Albee Mathews, 1951.

Mattoon, Annie. 'We Went to Haifa'. Unpublished article.

Maxwell, May. *An Early Pilgrimage*. Oxford: George Ronald, 1953.

Nakhjavani, Violette. *Amatu'l-Bahá Visits India*. New Delhi: Bahá'í Publishing Trust (no date).

National Programming Committee. Story supplement for *God Passes By*. Wilmette, Illinois: Bahá'í Publishing Committee, 1948.

Pattern of Bahá'í Life, The. A compilation from Bahá'í Scripture with some passages from the writings of the Guardian of the Bahá'í Faith. London: Bahá'í Publishing Trust, reprinted 1970.

Pemberton, L. B. *A Modern Pilgrimage to Palestine.* Philadelphia: Dorrance and Company, 1925.

Phelps, M. H. *Abbas Effendi, His Life and Teachings.* Introduced by ✓ E. G. Browne. New York: G. P. Putnam's Sons, 1912.

Rabbani, Rúḥíyyih. *The Priceless Pearl.* London: Bahá'í Publishing Trust, 1969.

'Report of the Eighteenth Annual Lake Mohonk Conference on International Arbitration.' Lake Mohonk Conference on International Arbitration, 1912.

'Roy' and M. J. M. *Knock and It Shall Be Opened Unto You.* (No details.)

✓ Ruhe, David. *Door of Hope.* A Century of the Bahá'í Faith in the Holy Land. Oxford: George Ronald, 1983.

Shoghi Effendi, *Advent of Divine Justice, The.* Wilmette, Illinois: Bahá'í Publishing Trust, 1971.

—— *God Passes By.* Wilmette, Illinois: Bahá'í Publishing Trust, 1974.

—— *World Order of Bahá'u'lláh, The.* Wilmette, Illinois: Bahá'í Publishing Trust, 1980.

—— *The Bahá'í Life.* Extracts from the Guardian's writings published by the National Spiritual Assembly of the Bahá'ís of Canada, 1973.

Star of the West. The Bahá'í Magazine. vols. II, III, IV, V, VI, VIII, IX, X, XI, XIII, XIV, XV, XVI, XVII, and XXIII. Published in USA between 1911 and 1933. vols. I–XIV reprinted in *Star of the West.* Oxford: George Ronald, 1978.

Taherzadeh, Adib. *The Revelation of Bahá'u'lláh.* vol. 2. Oxford: George Ronald, 1977.

Thompson, Juliet. *'Abdu'l-Bahá, The Center of the Covenant.* Wilmette, Illinois: Bahá'í Publishing Committee, 1948.

—— *Abdul Baha's First Days in America.* New York: The Roycrofters (no date).

Townshend, George. *The Mission of Bahá'u'lláh.* Oxford: George Ronald, 1973.

True, Corinne. *Notes Taken at Acca.* Chicago, Illinois: Baha'i Publishing Society, 1907.

Universal House of Justice. *Messages from the Universal House of Justice, 1968–1973.* Wilmette, Illinois: Bahá'í Publishing Trust, 1976.

BIBLIOGRAPHY

Universal House of Justice. *Wellspring of Guidance*. Wilmette, Illinois: Bahá'í Publishing Trust, 1970.

Vajdi, K. H. *Human Happiness*. India: K. H. Vajdi (no date).

Ward, Allan L. *239 Days: 'Abdu'l-Bahá's Journey in America*. Wilmette, Illinois: Bahá'í Publishing Trust, 1979.

World Order. Wilmette, Illinois: National Spiritual Assembly of the Bahá'ís of the United States, Fall 1971.

REFERENCES

PREFACE

1. 'Abdu'l-Bahá, *Selections from the Writings of* , pp. 245–6.
2. Shoghi Effendi, *The Advent of Divine Justice*, p. 29.
3. Universal House of Justice, *Wellspring of Guidance*, p. 97.
4. Universal House of Justice, *Messages from the Universal House of Justice*, p. 25.
5. Universal House of Justice, *Bahá'í News*, No. 517, April 1974, p. 2.
6. Jordan, *The Meaning of Deepening*, p. 58.
7. Shoghi Effendi, *The World Order of Bahá'u'lláh*, p. 5.
8. 'Abdu'l-Bahá, *Tablets of 'Abdu'l-Bahá*, vol. I, p. 190.
9. *The Magazine of the Children of the Kingdom*, June 1924, p. 50.

INTRODUCTION

1. Esslemont, *Bahá'u'lláh and the New Era*, p. 64.
2. Shoghi Effendi, *God Passes By*, p. 245.
3. ibid. p. 246.
4. ibid. p. 283.
5. ibid. p. 289.
6. ibid. p. 267.
7. ibid. p. 325.
8. Blomfield and Shoghi Effendi, *The Passing of 'Abdu'l-Baha*, p. 10.
9. Shoghi Effendi, *God Passes By*, p. 243.

I. HIS PURE HEART

1. 'Abdu'l-Bahá, *Selections from the Writings of* , p. 10.
2. *Abdul Baha in London*, p. 110.
3. Hofman, *The Renewal of Civilization*, p. 33.
4. Blomfield, *The Chosen Highway*, p. 166.
5. *Bahá'í World*, vol. XIII, p. 1187.
6. Holley, *Religion for Mankind*, p. 229.
7. *The Pattern of Bahá'í Life*, p. 18.

8. Ives, *Portals to Freedom*, p. 71.
9. *Star of the West*, vol. V (1913–1914), p. 40.
10. Blomfield, *The Chosen Highway*, p. 136.
11. Goodall and Cooper, *Daily Lessons Received at Acca, January 1908*, pp. 73–4.
12. Maxwell, *An Early Pilgrimage*, p. 42.
13. *Bahá'í World*, vol. IV, p. 384.
14. Ives, *Portals to Freedom*, p. 194.
15. ibid. pp. 47–9.
16. Phelps, *Abbas Effendi, His Life and Teachings*, pp. 101–2.
17. Ward, *239 Days: 'Abdu'l-Bahá's Journey in America*, p. 190.
18. Cited *Bahá'í World Faith*, pp. 448–9.
19. ibid. p. 442.
20. *Bahá'í World*, vol. IV, p. 340.
21. ibid.
22. Esslemont, *Bahá'u'lláh and the New Era*, p. 75.
23. Blomfield, *The Chosen Highway*, p. 214.
24. Ferraby, *All Things Made New*, p. 237.
25. *Bahá'í World*, vol. IV, p. 339.
26. *Child's Way*, July–August 1973, pp. 9–10.
27. Mathews, *Not Every Sea Hath Pearls*, pp. 39–40.
28. *Bahá'í World*, vol. IV, p. 340.
29. *Star of the West*, vol. IV, p. 120.
30. Ives, *Portals to Freedom*, pp. 39–40.
31. Taherzadeh, *The Revelation of Bahá'u'lláh*, vol. 2, p. 45.
32. *Star of the West*, vol. XIII, p. 141.
33. Lucas, *A Brief Account of My Visit to Acca*, pp. 28–9.
34. Blomfield, *The Chosen Highway*, p. 156.
35. Grundy, *Ten Days in the Light of Acca*, p. 73. The Master's recipe for pilau: *Lamb* – cut in very small pieces – cutting away all fat, bone, gristle. Put *butter* in frying pan and when it bubbles, stir in the meat and continue to stir constantly until the meat is done. Season with *salt. Raisins* – look them over and wash them. Cook with equal amount of *Syrian Pine nuts* – in another frying pan in same manner as lamb – in butter – stir nuts and raisins constantly. When ready to serve, mix most of nuts and raisins with the meat, using more meat than nuts and raisins. Place this mixture in the center of a serving platter and arrange a border of cooked *rice* around it, using the remaining nuts and raisins as decoration, according to taste.
36. Maxwell, *An Early Pilgrimage*, pp. 23–5.
37. *Bahá'í World*, vol. IV, p. 339.

38. Phelps, *Abbas Effendi, His Life and Teachings*, p. 103.
39. Faizí, *Milly – A Tribute to Amelia E. Collins*, p. 7.
40. Chase, *In Galilee*, pp. 33–4.
41. Gail, *The Sheltering Branch*, p. 75.
42. ibid. p. 101.
43. Balyuzi, *'Abdu'l-Bahá*, pp. 32–3.
44. Phelps, *Abbas Effendi, His Life and Teachings*, p. 78.
45. *Bahá'í World*, vol. XII, p. 704.
46. Blomfield and Shoghi Effendi, *The Passing of 'Abdu'l-Baha*, pp. 30–1.
47. Cobb, *Memories of Abdu'l-Bahá*, pp. 5–6.
48. *Star of the West*, vol. XIII, p. 143.
49. Shoghi Effendi, *God Passes By*, pp. 275–6.
50. *Bahá'í News*, September 1977, p. 6. from *The Wondrous Annals*, Mírzá Maḥmúd-i-Zarqání.
51. *Bahá'í World*, vol. IX, p. 806.
52. Balyuzi, *'Abdu'l-Bahá*, p. 37.
53. Adapted from Pemberton, *A Modern Pilgrimage to Palestine*, pp. 99–100.
54. 'Abdu'l-Bahá, *Tablets of Abdul-Baha*, vol. II, p. 303.
55. 'Abdu'l-Bahá, *Promulgation of Universal Peace*, vol. I, p. 67.
56. *Star of the West*, vol. IV, p. 207.

II. HIS KINDLY HEART

1. 'Abdu'l-Bahá, *Paris Talks*, p. 16. Also, *Divine Art of Living*, p. 115.
2. Shoghi Effendi, *God Passes By*, p. 283.
3. Ives, *Portals to Freedom*, p. 84.
4. *Star of the West*, vol. XIV, pp. 365–7.
5. McDaniel, *The Spell of the Temple*, pp. 16–17.
6. Blomfield, *The Chosen Highway*, p. 101.
7. Phelps, *Abbas Effendi, His Life and Teachings*, p. 107.
8. *Star of the West*, vol. IV, p. 205.
9. 'Abdu'l-Bahá, *Promulgation of Universal Peace*, vol. I, pp. 199–200.
10. Rabbani, *The Priceless Pearl*, p. 8.
11. Gail, *The Sheltering Branch*, pp. 70–1.
12. Balyuzi, *'Abdu'l-Bahá*, pp. 33–4.
13. Thompson, *'Abdu'l-Bahá – The Center of the Covenant*, pp. 19–20.

14. 'Abdu'l-Bahá, *Promulgation of Universal Peace*, vol. I, p. 89.
15. Blomfield, *The Chosen Highway*, p. 159.
16. ibid. pp. 162–3 (adapted).
17. *Bahá'í World*, vol. XII, p. 689.
18. *Star of the West*, vol. VIII, p. 6.
19. Blomfield, *The Chosen Highway*, pp. 161–2.
20. Bahá'u'lláh, *The Hidden Words* (Persian), No. 36.
21. Goodall and Cooper, *Daily Lessons Received at Acca*, pp. 67–8.
22. 'Abdu'l-Bahá, *Paris Talks*, p. 35.
23. Blomfield, *The Chosen Highway*, p. 152.
24. *Bahá'í World*, vol. XIII, p. 1187.
25. ibid. vol. XI, p. 491.
26. Thompson, *Abdul-Baha's First Days in America*, p. 19.
27. Bahíyyih Ford, Notes of (unpublished, see reference 75).
28. Ford, *The Oriental Rose*, pp. 94–9.
29. Maxwell, *An Early Pilgrimage*, pp. 25–6.
30. Ives, *Portals to Freedom*, pp. 36–7.
31. *Star of the West*, vol. VIII, p. 4.
32. Vajdi, *Human Happiness*, p. 54.
33. Blomfield, *The Chosen Highway*, pp. 211–12 (adapted).
34. *Star of the West*, vol. VIII, pp. 4–5.
35. 'Abdu'l-Bahá, *Paris Talks*, pp. 114–15.
36. Shoghi Effendi, *God Passes By*, p. 282.
37. Balyuzi, *'Abdu'l-Bahá*, p. 100.
38. *Star of the West*, vol. XV, No. 3, p. 74. Also vol. XIII, pp. 271–2.
39. ibid.
40. *Bahá'í World*, vol. IV, pp. 208–10.
41. *Report of the Eighteenth Annual Lake Mohonk Conference on International Arbitration*, pp. 42–4 (note).
42. *Bahá'í News*, April 1973, p. 6.
43. Blomfield, *The Chosen Highway*, p. 157.
44. Phelps, *Abbas Effendi, His Life and Teachings*, pp. 108–9.
45. *Star of the West*, vol. VIII, p. 5.
46. Ford, *The Oriental Rose*, p. 165.
47. Phelps, *Abbas Effendi, His Life and Teachings*, p. 7.
48. ibid. (adapted), pp. 103–4.
49. *Star of the West*, vol. IX, pp. 193–4.
50. Phelps, *Abbas Effendi, His Life and Teachings*, p. 5.
51. Blomfield, *The Chosen Highway*, p. 101.
52. Lucas, *A Brief Account of My Visit to Acca*, p. 29.
53. *Star of the West*, vol. X, pp. 218–19.
54. Ferraby, *All Things Made New*, p. 236.

55. 'Abdu'l-Bahá, *Promulgation of Universal Peace*, vol. I, pp. 30–1.
56. *Star of the West*, vol. VIII, pp. 5–6.
57. Thompson, *Abdul-Baha's First Days in America*, p. 11.
58. True, *Notes Taken at Acca*, pp. 22–3 (adapted).
59. ibid. p. 24.
60. Roy, *Knock and It Shall Be Opened Unto You*, p. 7.
61. Lucas, *A Brief Account of My Visit to Acca*, p. 28.
62. Roy, *Knock and It Shall Be Opened Unto You*, p. 1.
63. ibid. pp. 5–6.
64. Ward, *239 Days: 'Abdu'l-Bahá's Journey in America*, p. 134.
65. Ives, *Portals to Freedom*, p. 129.
66. 'Abdu'l-Bahá, *Selections from the Writings of*, p. 24.
67. ibid. p. 34.
68. Shoghi Effendi, *God Passes By*, pp. 317–18.
69. Balyuzi, *'Abdu'l-Bahá*, pp. 92–3.
70. Blomfield, *The Chosen Highway*, pp. 137–9.
71. ibid. p. 142.
72. *Bahá'í News*, September 1977, p. 5.
73. Grundy, *Ten Days in the Light of 'Akká*, p. 103.
74. Maxwell, *An Early Pilgrimage*, pp. 14–16.
75. Based on typed notes sent by Bahíyyih Randall Ford (Winckler) from S. Africa.
76. *Star of the West*, vol. III, No. 4, p. 29. Quoted in *Bahá'í News*, September 1977, p. 6.
77. *Star of the West*, vol. IX, p. 28.
78. Blomfield, *The Chosen Highway*, pp. 159–60 (adapted).
79. Shoghi Effendi, *God Passes By*, p. 311.
80. Blomfield and Shoghi Effendi, *The Passing of 'Abdu'l-Bahá*, p. 8.
81. Gail, *The Sheltering Branch*, p. 43.
82. Ives, *Portals to Freedom*, p. 116.
83. Lucas, *A Brief Account of My Visit to Acca*, p. 15.
84. True, *Notes Taken at Acca*, pp. 29–30.
85. Roy, *Knock and It Shall Be Opened Unto You*, p. 1.
86. Based on typed notes sent by Bahíyyih Randall Ford (Winckler) from S. Africa.
87. 'Abdu'l-Bahá, *Paris Talks*, p. 38.
88. *Star of the West*, vol. XIII, No. 6, p. 144.
89. Esslemont, *Bahá'u'lláh and the New Era*, p. 83.
90. Faizi, *The Bahá'í Faith – An Introduction*, pp. 55–6.
91. Blomfield, *The Chosen Highway*, p. 171.
92. Ford, *The Oriental Rose*, p. 6.

93. Blomfield, *The Chosen Highway*, pp. 161–2.
94. *Bahá'í World*, vol. XII, p. 920.
95. 'Abdu'l-Bahá, *'Abdu'l-Bahá in Canada*, p. 57.
96. *Child's Way*, July–August 1973, pp. 7–9.
97. Balyuzi, *'Abdu'l-Bahá*, p. 390.
98. Lucas, *A Brief Account of My Visit to Acca*, p. 16.
99. Balyuzi, *'Abdu'l-Bahá*, p. 437.
100. *Star of the West*, vol. II, No. 14, p. 11.
101. Ives, *Portals to Freedom*, pp. 64–7 (adapted).
102. Maxwell, *An Early Pilgrimage*, p. 20.
103. Shoghi Effendi, *God Passes By*, p. 259.
104. Ives, *Portals to Freedom*, p. 52.
105. ibid. p. 53.
106. ibid. pp. 242–3.
107. Ives, *Portals to Freedom*, pp. 84–5.
108. Ruhe, *Door of Hope*, Ch. 4.
109. Blomfield, *The Chosen Highway*, p. 169.
110. Ward, *239 Days: 'Abdu'l-Bahá's Journey in America*, p. 64.
111. Bahá'u'lláh, *The Hidden Words* (Arabic), No. 2.
112. 'Abdu'l-Bahá, *Paris Talks*, p. 159.
113. Nakhjavani, *Amatu'l-Bahá Visits India*, p. 129.
114. 'Abdu'l-Bahá, *The Secret of Divine Civilization*, p. 40.
115. *Star of the West*, vol. XVI, p. 528.
116. Austin, *The Story of Louis G. Gregory*, p. 12.
117. Ward, *239 Days: 'Abdu'l-Bahá's Journey in America*, p. 74.
118. Austin, *The Story of Louis G. Gregory*, pp. 11–12. Also, *Bahá'í World*, vol. XII, p. 668. (Versions differ slightly.)
119. Austin, *The Story of Louis G. Gregory*, pp. 7–8.
120. Balyuzi, *'Abdu'l-Bahá*, pp. 317–18.
121. 'Abdu'l-Bahá, *Selections from the Writings of*, pp. 96–7.
122. *Star of the West*, vol. V, p. 216.
123. ibid. vol. XIII, No. 6, p. 143.
124. Ward, *239 Days: 'Abdu'l-Bahá's Journey in America*, pp. 175–6.
125. Shoghi Effendi, *The World Order of Bahá'u'lláh*, p. 37.
126. National Programming Committee, Story Supplement for *God Passes By*, p. 57.
127. 'Abdu'l-Bahá, *The Promulgation of Universal Peace*, vol. II, p. 349.
128. 'Abdu'l-Bahá, *Selections from the Writings of*, p. 200.
129. ibid. p. 129.
130. ibid. pp. 153–4.
131. ibid. p. 267.

132. ibid. p. 311.
133. Holley, *Religion for Mankind*, p. 236.
134. *Star of the West*, vol. IX, p. 201.
135. *Bahá'í News*, September 1970, p. 7.
136. *Star of the West*, vol. XII, No. 11, p. 177.
137. 'Abdu'l-Bahá, *The Promulgation of Universal Peace*, vol. I, p. 213.
138. 'Abdu'l-Bahá, *Will and Testament*, see *Bahá'í World Faith*, p. 449.
139. *Star of the West*, vol. XI, p. 43.
140. Grundy, *Ten Days in the Light of 'Akká*, p. 40.
141. *The Divine Art of Living*, p. 9.
142. 'Abdu'l-Bahá, *Tablets of Abdul-Baha Abbas*, vol. II, p. 274.
143. 'Abdu'l-Bahá, *The Promulgation of Universal Peace*, vol. I, p. 127.
144. Grundy, *Ten Days in the Light of 'Akká*, p. 13.
145. *Bahá'í World*, vol. XIII, p. 847.
146. Ward, *239 Days: 'Abdu'l-Bahá's Journey in America*, p. 168.
147. Shoghi Effendi, *God Passes By*, p. 259.
148. Esslemont, *Bahá'u'lláh and the New Era*, p. 75.
149. Mattoon, 'We Went to Haifa' (Mimeographed copy), p. 9.

III. HIS RADIANT HEART

1. 'Abdu'l-Bahá, *Paris Talks*, p. 15.
2. ibid. p. 113.
3. *The Divine Art of Living*, p. 70. Also *Bahá'í World*, vol. IV, p. 384.
4. Bahá'u'lláh, *Gleanings from the Writings of*, p. 303.
5. 'Abdu'l-Bahá, *Paris Talks*, p. 110.
6. Cobb, *Memories of Abdul-Bahá*, p. 6.
7. Brown, *Memories of 'Abdu'l-Bahá*, p. 38.
8. *Messages from Abdul-Baha – To the Honolulu Bahais*, pp. 3–4.
9. 'Abdu'l-Bahá, *Paris Talks*, pp. 109–10.
10. 'Abdu'l-Bahá, *Selections from the Writings of*, p. 211.
11. ibid. pp. 203–4.
12. ibid. p. 92.
13. ibid. p. 175.
14. *Compilation on Bahá'í Education*, p. 27.
15. ibid. p. 26.

16. *The Divine Art of Living*, p. 18.
17. Brown, *Memories of 'Abdu'l-Bahá*, p. 47.
18. Ward, *239 Days: 'Abdu'l-Bahá's Journey in America*, p. 94.
19. 'Abdu'l-Bahá, *The Promulgation of Universal Peace*, vol. I, p. 213.
20. *Bahá'í News*, September 1977, p. 7.
21. Fathea'zam, *The New Garden*, p. 81.
22. *Bahá'í Prayers*, pp. 75–6 (UK edn).
23. Shoghi Effendi, *God Passes By*, p. 258.
24. Goodall and Cooper, *Daily Lessons Received at Acca, January 1908*, pp. 8–9.
25. *Star of the West*, vol. VIII, p. 38.
26. Ford, *The Oriental Rose*, pp. 211–12.
27. *Bahá'í World*, vol. IV, p. 338.
28. *Bahá'í World Faith*, p. 367.
29. ibid. p. 366.
30. Adapted from notes from Mr Randall's daughter, Bahíyyih Ford (Winckler).
31. Blomfield, *The Chosen Highway*, pp. 183–4.
32. Cobb, *Memories of Abdul-Bahá*, pp. 16–17.
33. 'Abdu'l-Bahá, *Abdul-Baha in London*, pp. 115–16.
34. 'Abdu'l-Bahá, *The Promulgation of Universal Peace*, vol. I, pp. 184–5 (both quotations).
35. *Bahá'í World*, vol. XIII, p. 1187.
36. Thompson, *Abdul-Baha's First Days in America*, pp. 39–40.
37. Grundy, *Ten Days in the Light of 'Akká*, p. 38.
38. ibid. pp. 38–9.
39. Haney, *A Heavenly Feast*, p. 18.
40. ibid. p. 11.
41. 'Abdu'l-Bahá, *Tablets of Abdul-Baha Abbas*, vol. III, p. 674.
42. *Star of the West*, vol. IV, No. 12, p. 208.
43. Shoghi Effendi, *The Bahá'í Life*, p. 3.
44. National Programming Committee, *Story Supplement*, p. 72.
45. Townshend, *The Mission of Bahá'u'lláh*, p. 48.
46. Grundy, *Ten Days in the Light of 'Akká*, pp. 85–6.
47. *The Divine Art of Living*, p. 26. Also *Star of the West*, vol. VIII, p. 44.
48. *The Divine Art of Living*, p. 31.
49. 'Abdu'l-Bahá, *Tablets of Abdul-Baha*, vol. III, pp. 683–4.
50. Baker, *The Path to God*, pp. 13–17.
51. 'Abdu'l-Bahá, *Abdul-Baha in London*, p. 97.

52. Lucas, *A Brief Account of My Visit to Acca*, p. 31.
53. *Star of the West*, vol. IX, p. 210.
54. Esslemont, *Bahá'u'lláh and the New Era*, pp. 90–1.
55. *World Order*, Fall 1971, p. 83.
56. Shoghi Effendi, *God Passes By*, pp. 266–8.
57. ibid. p. 267.
58. ibid. p. 269.
59. 'Abdu'l-Bahá, *Selections from the Writings of*, p. 242.
60. 'Abdu'l-Bahá, *Abdul-Baha in London*, p. 124.
61. Shoghi Effendi, *God Passes By*, pp. 269–70.
62. 'Abdu'l-Bahá, *Abdul-Baha in London*, p. 123.
63. Shoghi Effendi, *God Passes By*, p. 271.
64. ibid.
65. Blomfield, *The Chosen Highway*, p. 184.
66. Townshend, *The Mission of Bahá'u'lláh*, p. 49.
67. *Star of the West*, vol. VI, pp. 90–1.
68. Blomfield, *The Chosen Highway*, pp. 173–4.
69. National Programming Committee, Story Supplement, pp. 58–9.
70. Blomfield, *The Chosen Highway*, p. 177.
71. Blomfield and Shoghi Effendi, *The Passing of 'Abdu'l-Bahá*, p. 9. Also Balyuzi, *'Abdu'l-Bahá*, p. 462.
72. *Star of the West*, vol. IX, p. 122.
73. ibid. p. 102.
74. *Bahá'í News*, August 1962, p. 3.
75. Ford, *The Oriental Rose*, pp. 212–13.
76. 'Abdu'l-Bahá, *Selections from the Writings of*, p. 129.
77. Balyuzi, *'Abdu'l-Bahá*, p. 9.
78. 'Abdu'l-Bahá, *Tablets of Abdul-Baha*, vol. II, p. 258.
79. ibid. p. 263.
80. 'Abdu'l-Bahá, *Will and Testament of*, Part 2, para. 1.
81. ibid. Part 2, para. 5.
82. Balyuzi, *'Abdu'l-Bahá*, p. 415.
83. Nakhjavani, *Amatu'l-Bahá Visits India*, p. 159.
84. *Star of the West*, vol. IX, No. 18, p. 208.
85. Ward, *239 Days: 'Abdu'l-Bahá's Journey in America*, p. 101.
86. 'Abdu'l-Bahá, *Promulgation of Universal Peace*, vol. I, p. 213.
87. Holley, *Religion for Mankind*, pp. 234–5.
88. Brown, *Memories of 'Abdu'l-Bahá*, pp. 78–9.
89. 'Abdu'l-Bahá, *Abdul-Baha in London*, pp. 120–1.
90. Thompson, *'Abdu'l-Bahá, the Center of the Covenant*, p. 10.
91. Balyuzi, *'Abdu'l-Bahá*, p. 31.

92. Ives, *Portals to Freedom*, pp. 119–20.
93. Esslemont, *Bahá'u'lláh and the New Era*, p. 77.
94. *Star of the West*, vol. XII, No. 13, p. 214.
95. *Bahá'í World*, vol. XII, p. 919.
96. ibid. p. 899.
97. Balyuzi, *'Abdu'l-Bahá*, p. 155.
98. ibid. p. 155.
99. Blomfield, *The Chosen Highway*, p. 169.
100. *Star of the West*, vol. V, p. 86.
101. *Bahá'í World*, vol. IV, p. 383.
102. Balyuzi, *'Abdu'l-Bahá*, p. 350.
103. Thompson, *Abdul-Baha's First Days in America*, p. 7.
104. *Star of the West*, vol. IV, p. 35.
105. ibid. vol. IX, p. 211.
106. Ward, *239 Days: 'Abdu'l-Bahá's Journeys in America*, p. 173.

EPILOGUE

1. *The Garden of the Heart*, p. 14.
2. National Programming Committee, Story Supplement, p. 36. Also *Star of the West*, vol. XXIII, p. 74.
3. Thompson, *'Abdu'l-Bahá, the Center of the Covenant*, pp. 21–2.
4. *Star of the West*, vol. II, No. 14, p. 9.
5. Shoghi Effendi, *God Passes By*, p. 291.
6. *Star of the West*, vol. XVII, p. 354.
7. *Bahá'í World*, vol. II, p. 272.
8. *Bahá'í World*, vol. XIII, p. 822.
9. *Bahá'í World*, vol. IV, p. 515.
10. ibid.
11. *Bahá'í News*, February 1974, p. 19.
12. *Bahá'í World*, vol. XIII, p. 808.
13. Balyuzi, *'Abdu'l-Bahá*, p. 515.
14. Shoghi Effendi, *God Passes By*, p. 290.
15. Letter to the author.
16. Gail, *The Sheltering Branch*, pp. 25–6.
17. *Bahá'í World*, vol. VI, pp. 626–7.
18. Holley, *Religion for Mankind*, pp. 232–3.
19. *Bahá'í World*, vol. XIII, p. 842.
20. ibid. vol. IX, p. 626.
21. Ives, *Portals to Freedom*, p. 55.
22. ibid. p. 128.

23. *Bahá'í World*, vol. IX, pp. 618–19.
24. ibid. p. 612.
25. ibid. vol. II, p. 129.
26. ibid. vol. XII, p. 671.
27. ibid. vol. IX, pp. 635–6.
28. Shoghi Effendi, *God Passes By*, pp. 313–14.
29. ibid. p. 312.
30. Balyuzi, *Edward Granville Browne and the Bahá'í Faith*, pp. 119–20.
31. *Bahá'í World*, vol. XIII, p. 804.
32. ibid. p. 806.
33. Maxwell, *An Early Pilgrimage*, p. 39.
34. ibid. p. 40.
35. ibid. pp. 41–2.

INDEX TO ANECDOTES

I. HIS PURE HEART

Selflessness
1. Self, the greatest prison.
2. Freedom, not a matter of place.
3. Satan, the insistent self.
4. Self, man's only enemy.
5. Self-love, a strange trait.
6. I, me, mine.
7. 'Abdu'l-Bahá, the selflessness of Christ.
8. The peacock – think of God's bounty, not yourselves.
9. Behold a candle.
10. Photographs of self – the light important, not the lamp.
11. A good listener.
12. No private carriage.
13. No use for diamond rings.
14. The disciples of Christ forgot themselves.

Humility
15. Cooking and serving food for others.
16. Visiting Bahá'u'lláh.
17. His attitude to knighthood.
18. Unnecessary ceremony.
19. Wilmette, no golden trowel.
20. The first shall be last – forming a Local Spiritual Assembly.
21. Why rivers flow into the ocean.
22. The Nineteen-Day Feast – make others happy.
23. He taught 'as if offering a gift to a king'.
24. Scholar hurt by praise.

Simplicity
25. Simplicity and love.
26. His sparse diet.
27. Supper sent to the needy.

28. London dinner simplified.
29. Served guests.
30. The hermit and Bahá'u'lláh.
31. No bridal gown.
32. Simplicity reigns in the Master's family.
33. Simplicity in teaching.

Cleanliness
34. Personal spotlessness.
35. Spotless surroundings.

Patience
36. The stolen coal.
37. Little by little, day by day.
38. I am patiently waiting.
39. Endure the unendurable.
40. Patience towards those who deny religion.

Fortitude
41. Building the Shrine of the Báb.
42. Enduring the hardships of travel.

Integrity
43. Acknowledged by the people of 'Akká.

Sincerity
44. The merchant who wanted to become a Bahá'í.

Purity
45. Be like a clear mirror.
46. Purity of heart.
47. Attitude to fashion.

II. HIS KINDLY HEART

Kindliness
1. He rode the rods.
2. Wilmette – the stone refused by the builder.
3. Caring for the ill.
4. The man with tuberculosis.

5. A broken leg.
6. Happiness – a great healer.

Discipline
7. Getting up in the morning.

Forgiveness
8. Forgive him now.
9. <u>Sh</u>ay<u>kh</u> Maḥmúd – forgive me.
10. Persian princes.
11. See with the sight of forgiveness.

Sensitivity
12. A heart has been hurt.
13. Two ladies from Scotland.
14. A flower from the Master.
15. 'Abdu'l-Bahá, You'll be late!
16. Unexpected guests.
17. Teach only those who wish to hear – the French girl.

Encouragement
18. The message of Krishna is love.
19. British workman – work is worship.
20. Ride in the Ship of God.
21. The heart may speak better than words.
22. Juliet Thompson – your heart teaches.
23. Study. Study. Study.

Gentleness
24. With the Egyptian merchant.
25. Speak no evil (May Maxwell).
26. Try your own way!

Sympathy and Understanding
27. He gave away His bed.
28. No spare night-robe.
29. We want our Father.
30. Poverty in London and New York.
31. Surprise at lack of sympathy.

Generosity
32. Sheep for the shepherds.

33. A rug to a poor Arab.
34. A rug for Bahá'u'lláh's Shrine.
35. A rug for Mohonk Mountain House.
36. The Master refused money.
37. Generosity to children.
38. Coat, too expensive.
39. The second cloak.
40. Gift criticized.
41. Tudor-Pole gives cloak.
42. Cloaks for the poor.
43. He gave away gifts.

Charity
44. Salvation Army and Bowery Mission.
45. Friday mornings in 'Akká.
46. The lame, the halt and the blind.

Sacrifice
47. Generous tips.
48. He gave away His trousers.

Magnanimity
49. Malice towards none.
50. To those who tried to humiliate Him.
51. Kindness to unkind Governor.
52. Present for dismissed Governor.
53. Prayer for the dead.
54. Be positive – Jesus and the dead dog.

Thoughtfulness
55. Meeting postponed – pilgrim feeling ill.

Consideration
56. Travel in comfort.
57. Disregard individual shortcomings.

Compassion
58. Attitude when teaching.
59. From thoughts of suicide to hope.

Concern
60. For health of others.

Courtesy and Graciousness
61. To daughter of a desert chief.
62. The most perfect gentleman.

Hospitality
63. The Master's household.
64. A martyr's widow given a home.
65. All religions meet in His home.

Tenderness
66. Ḥaydar-'Alí.

Love
67. What it means to be a Bahá'í.
68. The soiled and crushed letter.
69. Deep love for friends.
70. In all He saw His Father's face.
71. Black bread and the shrivelled apple.
72. Flowers with love.
73. Roses for minister.
74. Rose for a child.
75. Love for children.
76. The Bedouin children.
77. Violets from the children.
78. Racial differences beautiful.
79. A heart white as snow.

Service, Commitment, Involvement
80. He never failed in small attentions.
81. Serve thy fellow man.
82. A simple wedding.
83. She's a perfect woman.
84. No special compartment on train.

Justice
85. Neither cheat nor be cheated.

Equality
86. Hotel integration.
87. A unity feast.
88. Evicted from hotel.

89. Integrating a Washington luncheon.
90. Interracial marriage encouraged.
91. Equality of men and women.

Moderation
92. The lady who gave her hair for the Temple.
93. Express yourself with moderation.
94. Even in thinking be moderate.
95. Too much austerity is not good.

Truthfulness
96. The principle of federalism.
97. Explore the invisibilities of the Kingdom.
98. Shall man fight for the tomb?
99. Surprising truths.

Knowledge and Wisdom
100. Constantine's mother.
101. Bahá'u'lláh pleased.
102. Seeing eyes and hearing ears.
103. Proving the validity of Islam.
104. How to teach.
105. Is last year's springtime sufficient?
106. Do not look at your weakness.
107. Make a beginning and all will come right.
108. A president should not hanker for the presidency.
109. Pilgrimages halted before World War I.
110. Never forget Christ.

III. HIS RADIANT HEART

Happiness
1. Are you happy? – Be happy!
2. Forget your sorrows.
3. His joyous words inspire.
4. Happiness and health.
5. Why so happy?
6. Glad tidings!
7. O God, refresh and gladden my spirit . . .

  8. Dry your tears.
  9. His heavenly smile.
 10. Be a strong ship.
 11. Why be happy?

Spirituality
 12. The intellect is good, but . . .
 13. With a Japanese ambassador.
 14. Do you teach the spiritual things?
 15. Encourage spirituality in children.
 16. For you I desire spiritual distinction.
 17. You were earthly, We wanted you heavenly.
 18. The material or the spiritual world?
 19. Happiness depends upon spiritual perception.
 20. Spiritual indigestion.
 21. Recite the Greatest Name.
 22. Spiritual perfection evolves but slowly.

Radiant Acquiescence
 23. Imprisoned in two prisons.

Prayerfulness
 24. Prayer in time of stress.
 25. Why pray?
 26. Prayer is indispensable.
 27. I will teach you to pray.
 28. Pray for the departed.
 29. Grace before meals.
 30. Prayer can be selfish.
 31. Service is prayer.

Equanimity and Imperturbability
 32. Shots fired in the night.
 33. Planting vines and trees.

Courage
 34. I shall not run away.
 35. Sticks of dynamite.
 36. Untroubled by danger.

Calm and Serenity
 37. In chains.

38. Unruffled in travel.
39. The *Titanic* – there is wisdom in it.
40. The most important before the important.
41. 'Abdu'l-Bahá's passing.

Trust
42. If God is willing.

Submission
43. No grief at death of son.

Devotion
44. Be on fire with the love of the Kingdom.
45. Talk to people about the love of God.

Contentment
46. Flour instead of bread.
47. The proof of nobility.
48. Sweeten their souls.
49. No shame in useful work.
50. Work gladly performed.
51. The bitter melon.
52. Richer than all the world.

Cheerfulness
53. Cheerful dining at Thonon-les-Bains.

Laughter
54. Making broth.
55. Laughter in chains.
56. Laughter – spiritual relaxation.
57. His home, a home of laughter.
58. Death, a messenger of joy.
59. We shall laugh together in the Kingdom.

Humour
60. So did Christopher Columbus.
61. Very difficult English words.
62. I am very young.
63. Comparing East and West.
64. Women in East and West.
65. Ladies of America and Europe.

66. No taxes in the Kingdom of God.
67. Importance of proper communication.
68. Grapes – and the need for a common language.
69. The banner of universal peace.

EPILOGUE

1. 'Abdu'l-Bahá – some tributes.
2. Treading the mystic way with practical feet.
3. Ludwig Zamenhof – founder of Esperanto.
4. Prof. E. G. Browne – a tribute.
5. The most important man in our century.
6. 'Abdu'l-Bahá's photograph.
7. Thieves and the Master.
8. The moon and 'Abdu'l-Bahá.
9. The Mystery of God.
10. Horace Holley by Lake Geneva.
11. George Townshend – the words of 'Abdu'l-Bahá.
12. Home in the Kingdom of God.
13. Once a Unitarian minister, then a pioneer.
14. 'Come down, Zachias.'
15. A fourteen-year-old girl.
16. Carole Lombard Gable.
17. The Governor of Phoenicia – an inspiration to hundreds and thousands.
18. A tribute from an Oxford professor.
19. 'A greater influence . . . than any Asiatic thinker and teacher of recent times.'
20. Queen Marie of Romania – 'A great light'.
21. Look at Me, follow Me, be as I am.